Praise for Patrick J. Mc(
FEAR OF MISSII

"As the creator of the term FOMO, Patrick J. ... to lead the fight against this very modern afflic... McGinnis shows us how to take back control of the way we live and work. It is a must-read for all of us who want to escape the anxiety of indecision, live with more intention, and thrive.

— Arianna Huffington, founder and CEO, Thrive Global

"Timely, practical, and insightful... In *Fear of a Missing Out*, McGinnis addresses one of the greatest barriers to happiness...and chronicles how it can hijack both your personal and professional lives. Then he shows you how to live life on your own terms instead of letting life happen to you."

—Shawn Achor, happiness researcher and *New York Times* bestselling author of *Big Potential* and *The Happiness Advantage*

"Whether it's life's trivial details or its major crossroads, decision-making can be stressful and all-consuming. In this timely and essential book, Patrick J. McGinnis shows you why it doesn't have to be that way."

—Kerry Kennedy, president of Robert F. Kennedy Human Rights and *New York Times* bestselling author

"Living in an age of unprecedented choice makes the thousands of decisions you face each day more complex than ever. Using the frameworks of FOMO and FOBO, McGinnis gives you a set of user-friendly tools to make smarter, better choices."

—Nir Eyal, bestselling author of *Hooked* and *Indistractable*

"This book is one you would be right to fear missing out on. A fascinating and fun read."
—Seth Stephens-Davidowitz, *New York Times* bestselling author of *Everybody Lies*

"Patrick J. McGinnis has written the right book for our fraught moment in time. Smart, careful, and a pleasure to read, *Fear of Missing Out* shows the reader not only what FOMO means and does but how we can learn to escape its clutches and pursue lives of meaning instead."

—Debora L. Spar, MBA Class of 1952 Professor of Business Administration, Harvard Business School

"In *Fear of Missing Out*, Patrick J. McGinnis shows us why we have FOMO and helps us discover what we actually want. Because if you know what you want, you aren't really missing out, then, are you?"

—Dr. Will Cole, leading functional medicine expert, IFMCP, DC, author of *The Inflammation Spectrum* and *Ketotarian*, and cohost of the *Goopfellas* podcast

"Patrick is a true innovator when it comes to helping you identify how (shockingly) much FOBO [Fear of a Better Option] messes with your relationships, business, and routine tasks…then he trains your anti-FOBO muscles. FOMO may get all the meme attention, but FOBO is the real enemy of choosing what shirt to wear, developing friendships that have value, or scaling your dream startup to an exit."

—Jack Kramer and Nick Martell, cohosts of Robinhood's podcast *Snacks Daily*

"*Fear of Missing Out* is an indispensable handbook for anyone who wants to spend each day actually living their life instead of wasting precious time on indecision. Patrick is both generous and genuine, which is a rare gift in this world."

—Cathy Heller, creator and host of the podcast *Don't Keep Your Day Job*

"Whether you're managing a Fortune 500 company, an entrepreneurial venture, or your day-to-day life, you will need to be resolute if you're going to succeed. This book provides easy to use yet powerful strategies to push past indecision and focus on what matters."

—Dorie Clark, executive education faculty, Duke University Fuqua School of Business, and author of *Entrepreneurial You* and *Reinventing You*

"After first coining FOMO, McGinnis invented FOBO (Fear of a Better Option) to describe an even more destructive set of behaviors. Now he's back with a clear, step-by-step, and powerful approach to help people stop looking over their shoulders and instead embrace the real and exciting possibilities before them."

—Jamie Metzl, leading futurist and bestselling author of *Hacking Darwin*

"It took me nearly dying five times to learn what Patrick so eloquently shares in this must-read book: we must find the power to choose what we actually want and the courage to miss out on the rest. He provides concrete guidance for how to do this (without needing to have the near-death experiences!). McGinnis carries an urgent message: Don't live with regret. Step one is to read this book."

—Dr. David Fajgenbaum, author of *Chasing My Cure* and Assistant Professor of Medicine at the University of Pennsylvania

FEAR OF MISSING OUT

Practical Decision-Making in a World of Overwhelming Choice

PATRICK J. McGINNIS

Photo Credits
Internal images © page xix, 1, 11, 29, 39, 47, 67, 69, 85, 101, 103, 111, 129, 141, 155, 175, 177, 195, 205, 211, Artemisia1508/Getty Images; page 7, Pete Souza, The Obama-Biden Transition Project, CC 3.0; page 8, Glenn Francis, www.PacificProDigital.com, CC BY-SA 3.0; page 8, Anirudh Koul, CC 2.0; page 8, The Hollywood Social Lounge, https://www.youtube.com/channel/UCOnIZHsNL28f1dI1vHG2gTw, CC 3.0; page 8, T.Voekler, CC BY-SA 3.0; page 9, David Shankbone, CC 3.0; page 75, PATRICK HERTZOG/Getty Images; page 75, Nguyen Trong Bao Toan/Getty Images; page 86, Benedetta Barbanti/EyeEm/Getty Images; page 197, TechCrunch, CC 2.0
Internal image on page 24 is available in the public domain in the United States of America.

Published by Sourcebooks
P.O. Box 4410, Naperville, Illinois 60567-4410
(630) 961-3900
sourcebooks.com

Library of Congress Cataloging-in-Publication data is on file with the publisher.

Printed and bound in the United States of America.
SB 10 9 8 7 6 5 4 3 2 1

To all the FOMO *sapiens, especially those who hail from the 02163.*

Contents

Introduction   ix

SECTION I

Fear and Indecision in an Overwhelming World   xix

Chapter 1: A Brief History of FOMO   1

Chapter 2: Your FOMO's Not Your Fault   11

Chapter 3: More Than a Meme   29

Chapter 4: The Other FO You Need to Know   39

Chapter 5: The Sad Tale of the Man Who Got Everything

He Wanted   47

SECTION II

The Hidden Cost of Fear   67

Chapter 6: The Billion-Dollar Business of FOMO   69

Chapter 7: FOBO, the Anti-Strategy   85

SECTION III

Decisive: Choosing What You Actually Want and

Missing Out on the Rest   101

Chapter 8: Freedom from Fear   103

Chapter 9: Don't Sweat the Small Stuff   111

Chapter 10: FOMO Is for the Planets, Not the Sun   129

Chapter 11: Choosing Action over Option Value   141

Chapter 12: Missing Out on the Rest   155

SECTION IV

Making FOMO and FOBO Work for You   175

Chapter 13: Going All In Some of the Time   177

Chapter 14: Game of FOs: Dealing with FOMO and FOBO

in Other People   195

EPILOGUE

We're Lucky to Have Options in the First Place   205

Author's Note   211

Acknowledgments   213

Notes   217

Index   227

About the Author   235

Introduction

The evolution of humanity from the dawn of time to the present day is not a subject without dispute. New discoveries upend existing theory and shift the known timeline of the development of our species by a couple of hundred thousand years this way or that. It's an inexact science, one that melds paleontology with genetics. Still, experts generally agree that about two million years ago, our first ancestor, *Homo habilis* (named for its use of stone tools), roamed Africa. Eventually, *Homo habilis* gave way to *Homo erectus*, and later *Homo sapiens*, which has dominated the earth ever since.

I'm here to announce a major new addition to the history of human evolution. While I'm not an archaeologist, I can assure you that there was no need to dig for fossils in rural Ethiopia to make the groundbreaking discovery that I'm about to share with you. There is ample evidence of this new form of human on the streets of New York, on the Tube in London, in the office buildings of Beijing, and at the coffee shops of São Paulo. Just as *Homo sapiens* displaced *Homo erectus*, modern humankind is itself giving way to a new species: *FOMO sapiens*.

You might be asking yourself how I can be so certain of this next stage of evolution. The short answer is that it takes one to know one.

My name is Patrick J. McGinnis, and I am the first known *FOMO sapiens*. I initially arrived at this realization way back in the early 2000s when I was a graduate student. But while I was the first of this new and curious species, I am certainly not the last. Today there are hundreds of millions, if not billions, of *FOMO sapiens*. Just as you could identify *Homo habilis* by its stone tools, *FOMO sapiens* exhibits a few tell-tale characteristics. In its natural habitat, *FOMO sapiens* can be observed yearning for all of the things, either real or imagined, that could make life *perfect*, if only it could have them or do them at this very moment. It's so distracted that if it had any natural predators, it would make for *shockingly* easy prey.

If you haven't heard of FOMO, let me catch you up. Do you ever get stressed out when you come across those delightful (read: highly selective, filtered, and cropped) photos posted by friends, family, and celebrities to your social media feed? As you scroll, you may notice that a feeling starts to build within you, perhaps best understood as a sense of anxiety. While you're playing with your phone, it occurs to you that all of these people are *living lives* that are far more interesting, exciting, successful, and, frankly, Instagramable than yours. This feeling is called **FOMO**, short for Fear of Missing Out, and its effects are widespread.

Contrary to popular belief, FOMO isn't just confined to what you see on social media. It runs much deeper, with implications that go far beyond shaping the daily lives of digital natives, such as millennials and Gen Z. Those two groups are naturally predisposed to evolve into *FOMO sapiens*, but their parents are clear candidates as well. FOMO hounds the middle-aged executive who is stuck in the office while his younger colleague gets invited to a conference in Vegas. It also pesters the sixty-year-old woman whose friends share so many details about their grandkids that she longs for her children to finally start having babies already. Social media heightens FOMO, but you don't need to be glued to your phone to fall into its trap. All you have to do is spend an inordinate amount of time and energy focused on all of the things that you *wish* you had rather than appreciating the things that you *do* have yet take for granted. The temptation to do so is increasingly prevalent given that so many people now live in a world that offers overwhelming choice, either real or perceived, for almost anything.

Before I go any further, I should come clean about something: the other reason I know that I was the first *FOMO sapiens* is that I'm the guy who came up with the term FOMO in the first place. In 2004, I introduced the acronym in an article titled "Social Theory at HBS: McGinnis' Two FOs" in *The Harbus*, the student newspaper of Harvard Business School (HBS). Now, over fifteen years later, that four-letter word has become a pretty big deal. It's appeared all over pop culture and it's even been added to a host of authoritative dictionaries, including the *Oxford English Dictionary* and Merriam-Webster. In my own life, the most tangible result of this distinction is that a lot of people want to take selfies with me. Naturally, they post them to social media in order to give all of their friends FOMO…if you think about it for too long, it's all pretty meta.

All selfies aside, I feel a little bit guilty for making FOMO *a thing*. Despite its popularity and extreme hashtagability, it is not a laughing matter. It causes stress, insecurity, jealousy, and even depression. It also imperils your success at work, tempts you to make speculative investments, and compels business leaders, from CEOs to start-up founders, to chase after the wrong strategies and squander precious resources. Put simply, it's a massive distraction and a waste of valuable time and energy.

And that's not the worst of it. I regret to inform you that FOMO isn't the only FO that you have to worry about. If you were paying close attention, you might have noticed that the article I wrote was subtitled "McGinnis' Two FOs." So, what happened to the other FO? While FOMO has gone on to fame and fortune, the other FO, well, at least until very recently, not so much.

FOBO, or Fear of a Better Option, is the anxiety that something better will come along, which makes it undesirable to commit to existing choices when making a decision. It's an affliction of abundance that drives you to keep all of your options open and to hedge your bets. As a result, you live in a world of maybes, stringing yourself and others along. Rather than assessing your options, choosing one, and moving on with your day, you delay the inevitable. It's not unlike hitting the snooze button on your alarm clock only to pull the covers over your head and fall back asleep. As you probably found out the hard way, if you hit snooze enough times, you'll end up being late and racing for the office, your day upended and your mood foul. While pressing snooze felt so good at the moment, it ultimately exacts a price.

FOBO is a serious problem that can inflict far more damage than FOMO. Unlike FOMO, which is largely an internal struggle, the costs of FOBO aren't just borne by you, they are also imposed on those around you. When you treat your life like a Tinder feed, swiping with reckless abandon without ever committing to any of the potential options, you turn everything around you, from opportunities to individuals, into commodities. You also send a clear and unambiguous message to everyone else: *you are the ultimate holdout*. You won't set a clear course or commit to a plan of action. Instead, you will let the possibilities pile up and only make a decision when it suits you, likely at the last minute, if at all. These personal defects can wreak havoc on your career trajectory, and they can translate into broader management challenges that imperil companies large and small by engendering analysis paralysis, stifling innovation, and robbing leaders of their authority.

It's no coincidence that I discovered FOBO at the exact same time as FOMO. If you are the kind of person who is prone to fear missing out, then you are also a likely candidate to compulsively keep your options open. The common thread between these two concepts—that you have many options and opportunities, either real or imagined—is very much a by-product of our modern tech-enabled age. But while most everyone now knows how to spot FOMO in their personal and professional lives, FOBO gets a free pass. It's hiding in plain sight.

It's time to acknowledge that when you live with the negative effects of FOMO or FOBO or both, you run the risk of blowing up your career, destroying your business, imperiling critical personal and professional relationships, and making yourself miserable in the process. Irrespective of these dire long-term consequences, the FOs can also creep into the mundane details of your daily life and seriously impact your productivity. They will then distract you, rob you of any clarity of purpose, and take you away from the present and into a tangled world of hypotheticals, calculations, and trade-offs. They will also sap you of conviction, consume your energy, and impair your performance. Each on its own is problematic, but taken together, they are catastrophic. When you combine FOMO and FOBO, you end up paralyzed with a critical case of FODA—Fear of Doing Anything.

Have you ever heard of the wounded healer? It's a personality archetype created by the psychologist Carl Jung to explain why some people become psychotherapists. Jung believed that many therapists choose their careers because their experiences as patients have given them a special vocation to help others dealing with the same kinds of issues. They may only be a few steps ahead of their patients on their own road to recovery, but having made those steps, they are uniquely positioned to help. I can relate to that. I like to think of myself as the world's first FOMOlogist. I've studied its causes, nature, and implications. More importantly, after fifteen years of living with FOMO and FOBO, I finally know how to manage them, although the struggle always continues.

Case in point, the words on this page were written during a sabbatical I took in Mexico City. Why did I set up shop in a different country and choose to work from a place that's more than 2,000 miles from home? As much as I'd like to claim it was for easy access to tacos and tequila, the reason is FOMO. Facing an all-consuming task, I knew that the risk of falling victim to the distractions of FOMO was way too high if I stayed home in New York City. With that decision behind me, I also managed pangs of FOBO when trying to settle on dates, lock down the optimal Airbnb, and find the coolest coffee shop in which to write. I made all of these decisions while fully aware of how FOMO and FOBO were driving my behavior. Then I relied on the strategies that I will show you in this book to overcome them.

My path to (relative) freedom from FOMO and FOBO has not been an easy one. I have spent my entire adult life living in New York City, a place that is home to millions of *FOMO sapiens* who think nothing of lining up for hours to experience the latest restaurant, the most buzzed-about exhibit, or some impossible-to-snag collaboration from the cult fashion-brand Supreme. I have also worked in an industry, venture capital, that is often driven by FOMO and FOBO and have traveled all over the globe, from Silicon Valley to Pakistan and Istanbul to Buenos Aires, in search of the hottest start-ups. Even when I've tracked them down, I've often been paralyzed at the moment when it was time to make those big bets. These bouts of indecision have cost me time, money, and focus, all to the detriment of my wallet and my well-being. It's only when I realized that my FOs were costing me money and peace of mind that I decided it was time to find ways to deal with them. In fact, these lessons from my career as a venture capitalist have informed a number of the decision-making strategies that you will learn in this book.

If you're here right now, I'm going to assume that you too are looking to conquer FOMO or FOBO. No matter your profession or stage of life, the antidote to these challenges is the same: you must learn to be *decisive*. When you are decisive, you strip away the fear from decision-making, remove the emotion from your deliberations, and take action. In doing so, you recognize that when you miss out on an opportunity, you don't necessarily limit your options. On the contrary, you give yourself freedom. Rather than letting life pass you by while you vacillate, you claim what you truly want out of life. You make things happen instead of letting life happen to you. You replace fear with conviction.

If all of that sounds great, then it's time to get to work. While the solutions to your FOs are within reach, living and working decisively is not something that happens overnight. In the same way that indecision slowly creeps into your subconscious, it will take you some time to deprogram yourself. You will do this by following a process that will be guided by two core principles:

1. **You will learn to choose what you actually want.** Rather than collecting every option and then wasting time and energy weighing all possible choices, you must instead decide: close all other paths, move forward, and don't look back in regret. When you do so, you will find that making decisions is a direct pathway to freedom, even in a world of overwhelming choice.

2. **You will find the courage to miss out on the rest.** If you stop trying to do and be everything, you can actually have it all—by not having it all. Rather than longing for what you're missing, you'll feel a profound sense of relief as soon as you put everything else to the side. You will revel in what you missed and instead re-direct your attention to all of the things that truly matter in life.

The book is organized into four parts. The first two sections will show you what drives FOMO and FOBO and then take you through how they can impact your career, your business, and your life. The third section will prepare you to go out into the real world and fight your FOs by giving you the tools you'll need to prevail. Finally, section four will help you to change the way you think about FOMO and FOBO in order to reframe them and then use them for your benefit. In addition to this book, you can always find additional tools, ideas, and resources at patrickmcginnis.com and on my podcast *FOMO Sapiens*.

As you learn to overcome FOMO and FOBO, you will see that the methodologies you will employ are different from other decision-making strategies you might have encountered in the past. That's because when you're dealing with the FOs, you are not caught between a rock and a hard place. Instead, you are operating from a position of abundance. In a very real sense, this is a good problem to have, even if it doesn't feel like it at the moment. If you can manage to break free from indecision, then you can partake in this abundance and benefit from the fact you do, in fact, have plenty of acceptable options. But to do so, you have to accept that you cannot have it all. Overcoming FOMO will require you to determine whether any of the many opportunities that you feel tempted to explore are actually worth pursuing. On the contrary, when you have FOBO, you already have more viable alternatives than you can handle. Your challenge is to choose just one and then move forward.

Before we begin, it's worth considering, even as you learn to manage them, whether either FOMO or FOBO has any redeeming qualities that are worth preserving. The answer, perhaps surprisingly, is yes. FOMO, when kept in check, can provide the inspiration to branch out, take a risk, or make a change in your life. Say you're working eighty-hour weeks in the corporate world and you feel pangs of FOMO when your former colleague, now an entrepreneur, raises millions of dollars on Kickstarter for her new venture. What can you learn from those feelings? Perhaps a lot. In that sense, I think of FOMO in the same way I think of drinking wine. When consumed in moderation, it has clear health benefits. Plus, it can help you to loosen your inhibitions a bit (*in vino veritas*) so that you can wander over to the edge of your comfort zone. As long as you don't drink to excess, you'll feel fine in the morning, and you'll be ready for your next adventure. Chapter 13 will show you how to harness FOMO for good in order to broaden your horizons and seek new experiences in a sustainable way.

FOBO, on the other hand, is like smoking cigarettes. It has no redeeming qualities and nothing good can come from it. First, it is highly addictive. Second, even if it feels good at the moment, it will inflict long-term damage to all aspects of your well-being. Worst of all, the secondary effects of FOBO are exactly like those of secondhand smoke. While you're focused on your own selfish needs, your vice hurts everyone around you too. That's why you need to devise strategies to cut it off at the source and act with conviction. You'll learn more about that later on.

OK, it's time. Your journey starts now. Your first step, ironically, is a decision: Are you going to turn the page, both literally and metaphorically, and get started? Turning the page means shutting down your FOMO and continuing forward with this journey (goodbye viral cat videos). It also means ignoring your FOBO (no browsing on Amazon for an even better book to read). For the next two hundred pages, you're going to stay right here, focused on the task at hand. That's how you're going to turn this page, the next one, and so on until you reach the back cover. That's what it means to be decisive.

FEAR AND INDECISION IN AN OVERWHELMING WORLD

"There is no more miserable human being than one in whom nothing is habitual but indecision."

—WILLIAM JAMES

CHAPTER 1

A Brief History of FOMO

"FOMO (fear of missing out) is the
enemy of valuing your own time."
—ANDREW YANG

The year was 2002, and I was a first-year student at Harvard Business School. Looking back, when I arrived in Boston to start classes, I considered myself to be a relatively high-functioning *Homo sapiens*. I had spent the last few years making decisions, important grown-up decisions, of the kind that had never been expected of me back in college. I had moved three times, worked at two companies, and invested in more than ten companies in my role as a venture capitalist. I'd learned to make some consequential decisions, both personally and professionally, and I'd managed to do so with surprisingly little drama. If you'd asked me at the time, I would have told you that I was getting pretty good at the whole *adulting* thing.

Admittedly, that was a simpler time, before anyone had ever heard of things like sexting or selfies. When I started business school, I had no social media. Nobody did. Social networking was in its infancy, although that was just about to change: little did I know it, but Mark Zuckerberg was working on the first version of Facebook less than a mile from my student apartment. Still, even in the absence of Facebook, Twitter, and all of the social networks that help to power the FOMO phenomenon today, something happened to me the minute I stepped on campus: all of the sudden and without warning, I was consumed by a persistent anxiety that no matter where I was or what I was doing, something better was happening elsewhere. This was a clear product of my new habitat. For the first time in my life, I was immersed in an intensely choice-rich environment where almost anything seemed possible. At the same time, I could never even hope to scratch the surface of what was on offer. All I had to do was compare myself to my peers—most of whom were happy to tell me how much they had on their plates—to know that I could never keep up.

Let me explain. Life at HBS was what I imagine it would be like to live life *inside* of a social network. Every overstuffed day was like a real-world mashup of LinkedIn, Facebook, Twitter, and Snapchat, even though none of those companies existed at the time. You lived in a self-obsessed bubble where news traveled at the speed of lightning, so your conversations and your brags (humble or otherwise) served as a proxy social network, performing many of the same functions as a news feed, a witty Instagram story, or a snarky tweet. This environment cultivated a pervasive fear of being left out of the action going on around you, especially if it could end up being *bigger, better, and brighter* than what you were doing at the moment. Even if you didn't have a name for such feelings, and my classmates and I didn't yet have one, you constantly struggled with them.

I, perhaps, suffered more than my peers. In retrospect, I was a natural candidate to become the world's first *FOMO sapiens*. I grew up in a small town in Maine, not unlike the kind of place you would find in a Stephen King novel. If you've never been to Maine, let me tell you a little about what people do there. They eat lobster. They take walks on the beach. They shovel snow. They go to L.L. Bean. It's a great place to grow up and to live, but it's not a particularly choice-rich environment. Life is relatively predictable—even comfortably so—and I was used to selecting from a sensible number of alternatives for most anything I could ever want or need.

All of that changed when I started life as an MBA candidate. Not only was I bombarded with choices, but I also felt quite sincerely that I shouldn't let this once-in-a-lifetime set of experiences pass me by. The way I saw it, if you weren't afraid of missing out, then you probably *were* missing out. To make sure I did not, I tried to do *everything*. On campus, I was ubiquitous. The only thing I didn't have a *fear of missing out* on was sleep. I participated in scores of clubs and attended an unending stream of social events, recruiting presentations, conferences, weekend trips, lectures, and, of course, classes. On weekdays, I dragged myself out of bed before 7:00 a.m. and collapsed well after midnight. Weekends were just as hectic. If you threw a rock at any event on campus, chances are that you would have hit me.

Given my desire to take part in essentially *everything*, my friends started to tease me that I'd probably show up at the opening of an envelope. They were right. I clearly suffered from a persistent anxiety that I would fail to take full advantage of anything happening around me, whether it was social, academic, or otherwise. In response, I told them to look in the mirror—they were no better. We were all so busy making sure that we wouldn't be left behind that we were spending a lot of time and energy on things that didn't actually reflect our true priorities.

Rather than doing things because they were going to make us happier or smarter, we instead did them because everybody else was doing them too. There was very little thought behind this behavior: when you say yes to everything, no deliberation is required.

Although my friends and I joked about it, the fear was very real. It was also so common in my life and in the lives of my peers that I decided to give it a name. As the frequent creator of my own slang and shorthand, I decided that this concept, this fear, deserved an acronym. I shortened "fear of missing out" to FOMO, introduced it into my vocabulary, and worked it into the shared lingo of my friend group. Just before graduation in May 2004, I wrote about my favorite new word in that now-fated article in the school newspaper. In a little over one thousand words, I skewered a campus culture that was permeated by FOMO.

While the piece became a hit on campus, my expectations for the acronym's long-term prospects were limited. In fact, I had much higher hopes for another word I'd recently created—McGincident—that I wanted to become the default description of anything someone in my family did that was funny, clever, or memorable. Then, slowly and entirely unbeknownst to me, FOMO took on a life of its own. Over the next decade, the story of FOMO and its quest for global domination actually became a full-fledged McGincident!

How FOMO Took over the World

Although I was completely unaware of what was happening at the time, I've now been able to piece together FOMO's trajectory as it spread slowly but steadily beyond the confines of my friends and classmates to all corners of the earth. The term first became popular with MBAs across the United States, who could easily relate to the concept and quickly adopted it into the common lingo that travels between schools. As *Businessweek* (now *Bloomberg Businessweek*) satirically reported in 2007:

> An epidemic has hit America's top MBA programs. At Harvard Business School, it's called FOMO: fear of missing out. Symptoms include a chronic inability to turn down invitations to any party, dinner, or junket attended by anyone who might be a valuable addition to one's network—no matter the cost.[1]

The next year, in the *New York Times* bestseller *Ahead of the Curve: Two Years at Harvard Business School*, author Philip Delves Broughton, who graduated two years after me, wrote that:

> The trick to HBS, the administration kept telling us, was not succumbing to FOMO. You had to choose exactly what you wanted to do and do it without fretting about what else was going on. I quelled my own FOMO by going to the library each day and reading the newspapers, trying to get my head as far away from the bubble as possible. But FOMO was a persistent stalker on campus, sowing poison in every mind.[2]

FOMO continued to gain traction on a growing number of campuses, and the newly graduated *FOMO sapiens* who spilled out into the world each May got jobs in industries like technology, consulting, and finance. When they arrived at their offices all over the country and the world, they brought FOMO with them and introduced it to a broader professional audience. At the same time, the proliferation of social media, mobile internet penetration, and digital marketing helped to introduce FOMO into general popular culture.

But while technological advancements have been indispensable to spreading FOMO far and wide, I'm also reminded of an old saying that's a favorite of finance types: correlation does not imply causation. As you will see in the next chapter, FOMO existed long before smartphones were invented, and it would persist even if you restricted your collection of gadgets to a first-generation PalmPilot. Technology has now weaponized a set of emotions that have been part of humanity since the days of *Homo habilis*. The electronic devices that you carry around with you have added fuel to a fire that has been burning for millennia and then set it ablaze as never before.

In fact, in many ways, FOMO is a postmodern version of a classic idiom that has long been part of American culture. Way back in 1913, the comic strip *Keeping Up with the Joneses* made its debut in the pages of the *New York Globe*. The strip, which ran for decades, satirized the misadventures of a social climber named Aloysius and his family in their struggles to keep pace with the exploits of their neighbors the Joneses. If you read it, you'll find that it's a chronicle of analog FOMO at its finest, with the typical plotline centering on Aloysius's wife's efforts to get him to wear pink socks, a red necktie, and green spats, just like his frenemy Mr. Jones. While I too have been known to sport a red necktie from time to time, there's a far more remarkable coincidence that binds Aloysius and me. His full name was Aloysius P. McGinis. So, while we're separated by one "n," it's clear that Aloysius and I have a lot in common. He was the first McGin(n)is to have FOMO, but he certainly wasn't the last.

FOMO, International Word Celebrity

Today, FOMO has permeated all strata of society. It's no longer a niche problem, but rather a mass-market affliction that can strike anyone. In recognition of this status, it was added to the *Oxford English Dictionary* in 2013 and then included in the *Merriam-Webster Unabridged Dictionary* three years later. As it's gone mass market, it's also gone global. By making headlines all over the world, it's become clear that FOMO is far from an American phenomenon. Over the past few years, Spain's *El País* ran a column chronicling the rise of "Generación 'fomo,'" [3] and *The Times of India* asked, "Is FOMO Making You Paranoid?"[4] Meanwhile, France's *Le Figaro* wondered if FOMO might just be the illness of the new century in "Le fomo, nouvelle maladie du siècle?"[5] while the Turkish newspaper *Daily Sabah* warned, "Hastalığın adı 'FOMO'! Siz de yakalanmış olabilirsiniz…" or "The name of the disease is 'FOMO'! You might get it…."[6] Yikes.

Today, a search for the term on Google yields over ten million results and #FOMO pops up hundreds of thousands of times on sites like Twitter and Instagram. It's also used widely across media, in advertisements, in bitmojis, and in countless daily conversations across the globe.

Barack Obama ✓
@BarackObama

No need for #FOMO. Enter now, for free, to meet the President: http://t.co/nTpkrVz1oV.

Jun 29, 2013 12:53 PM

 **Khloé** ✔
@khloekardashian

I'm having major FOMO! My entire family is in NYC but I couldn't go due to shooting Kocktails. I might have to hop on a flight after taping

Feb 11, 2016 3:49 AM

 Backstreet Boys ✔
@backstreetboys

How many days until we're cruising? #FOMO #BSBCRUISE2016

Oct 8, 2015 5:33 PM

 Trevor Noah ✔
@Trevornoah

Everyone is saying Fomo. What is Fomo? I need to know so I can join in. Please help me.

Nov 13, 2012 6:05 AM

 **Harley-Davidson** ✔
@harleydavidson

#SturgisOrBust! The 78th @SturgisRally has been nothing but rolling thunder in the #BlackHills. If you aren't here, get here. The #FOMO is real. #HarleyDavidson #FindYourFreedom

Aug 5, 2018

Tyra Banks ✔
@tyrabanks

Today is the day! Register for #FierceUp now, or forever hold your #FOMO. @nyledimarco http://bit.ly/29ZeOKx

Jul 28, 2016

Simply put, FOMO is now an international word celebrity, used by paupers, presidents, and Kardashians alike. Given its power, it now lies at the center of a global conspiracy to influence your decisions that is driven by influencers, brands, and even your fellow *FOMO sapiens*. Ironically, although the Kardashians of the world are very much part of this machine, they are also beholden to it, just like you and me. As you'll see in the next chapter, almost no one, except for a few resolute and impenetrable souls, can truly escape its grasp.

CHAPTER 2

Your FOMO's Not Your Fault

"Fyre Festival looks set to be the biggest FOMO-inducing event of 2017."

—FYRE FESTIVAL INVESTOR PITCH DECK[1]

In April 2017, Fyre Festival—a can't-miss music event—crashed onto the collective consciousness for all the wrong reasons. The festival, which was backed by entrepreneur Billy McFarland and raptrepreneur Ja Rule, was to be held on Pablo Escobar's private island in the Bahamas. In order to sell tickets, the organizers bet all of their chips on an elite group of social media personalities. Dubbed Fyre Starters, these influencers targeted millennials, nearly half of whom admit that they attend live events so that they'll have something epic to share on social media.[2] The Fyre Starters included four of the biggest influencers of the moment: Kendall Jenner, Emily Ratajkowski, and the Bellas (Thorne and Hadid), with approximately 150 million Instagram followers among them.

Led by these Four Horse(wo)men of the Social Media Apocalypse, the Fyre Starters reached over 300 million people and enticed their followers to pony up as much as $12,000 per ticket. It worked. Within forty-eight hours of launch, 95 percent of the tickets were gone.[3] Yet despite promises of the weekend of a lifetime, Fyre Fest ended up being a made-for-social-media dumpster fire. I mean, Fyre. It turns out that when you're planning an international music festival, big dreams and the backing of Ja Rule are not enough. You need infrastructure. By the time the first guests arrived, it was clear that the show would not go on due to severe problems with security, food, and shelter. Plus, Blink-182 pulled out. Let that sink in.

Ironically, the festival that was built on the back of an army of online royalty was torn down by a rogue band of attendees whose posts went viral. As #FyreFestival trended, it became clear that the entire affair was designed from inception—from claiming to be taking over Escobar's island to promising gourmet food and luxury accommodations—to generate and monetize FOMO. It was cynical and it was excessive, but it was also a conspiracy: McFarland was eventually sentenced to six years in prison for his actions.

If you are tempted to roll your eyes or shake your head as you think about the lunacy that was Fyre Fest, you are not alone. Most people would never dream of dropping a small fortune because the Bellas posted something on Instagram. The entire incident seems foolish or farcical at best. Yet every day, in much smaller and far more subtle ways, you face your own personal Fyre Fest. Whether it's passing up a social event to stay late at work, trying not to pick up your phone at the dinner table, or wondering why everyone seems to be getting rich on bitcoin while you have no idea what a bitcoin does, you are constantly bombarded with triggers, both online and IRL (in real life) that tap into your subconscious and hijack your intuition. FOMO is pervasive whether you realize it or not.

Given this reality, the first step to beating FOMO is to learn to spot all of these small assaults on your attention and intention. To do so, you'll first need to understand how FOMO works and what it means. That's actually more difficult than it might seem. As the term has grown in popularity, so has the litany of definitions ascribed to it. For the purposes of clarity, I'd like to offer my own comprehensive definition of FOMO that will frame how we use and discuss the term from here onward.

FOMO

\'fō-(ˌ)mō\ Noun. Informal

1. Unwanted anxiety provoked by the perception, often aggravated via social media, that others are having experiences that are more satisfying than yours. **2.** Social pressure resulting from the realization that you will miss out on or be excluded from a positive or memorable collective experience.

The Role of Perception

Your impression of something's intrinsic value is based on all kinds of internal and external cues, things like family, friends, social media influencers, past experiences, and interests or passions. These are the elements that convince you that you just *have* to do or have something. They are not quantitative in nature but are instead shaded, at least in part, by feelings, biases, hopes, and insecurities. In a very fundamental sense, perception is a product of calculations that are highly emotional. When you feel FOMO in this way, your core impulse is centered on improving your condition. What makes you want to get off the couch and chase after that party, trip, baby, or job is a belief that in doing so, your life will be better in some way than it is right now. At its core, FOMO is *aspirational* in nature, rooted in a search for whatever's *bigger, better, and brighter* than your current surroundings. It also implicitly assumes that you have choices, perhaps even an overwhelming number of choices, either real or perceived, at your disposal.

At the same time, perception can also be deception. If you think about it, you really have no idea whether something is going to live up to its billing. The disconnect between what you think or hope you might get and what you'll actually get, which is known as an *asymmetry of information*, is woven directly into the DNA of FOMO. When you remember that the external influences that are trying to get you to do something are clouded, and potentially distorted, by an asymmetry of information, that's where things get interesting. You would not spend a minute of time or burn a single calorie worrying about missing out on something if you already knew what you'd get. Instead, you'd just say yes or pass. With perfect information, the unknown loses its power. If you've ever participated in online dating or shopped for real estate, where reality never quite lives up to the pictures, then you know what I'm talking about. When you compare perception with reality, the difference can be shocking. That's why social media influencers have a perverse incentive to make sure that whatever they're hawking looks amazing even if it's actually pretty meh. The minute that the asymmetry of information is removed, the jig is up.

The Role of Inclusion

As you'll see later in this chapter, humans are biologically hardwired to seek inclusion and to avoid exclusion at all costs. While this instinct was historically a manifestation of the rigors of the survival of the fittest, it has now morphed into something else: it's a desire to feel part of the group and to be in the know. Basically, it's the emotional equivalent of picking teams back in gym class when you were a kid. While you stood against the wall, the captains picked from among your classmates, going one by one, until they got to the last unlucky two to be called. If you weren't a very good athlete (I wasn't, thanks to more than a few extra pounds), then your greatest fear was to be selected last (I usually was). All I wanted, as I stood there looking down at my Nikes, was to feel included. If you've ever found yourself in that place, then you know what I'm talking about. You don't need to win the game, you don't even care if you score a point, but you just don't want to be left behind.

America's Running of the Bulls

While defining FOMO is helpful, the best way to talk about it is to illustrate how it lives and breathes in the real world. While there are lots of case studies out there, I'm convinced that someday, when psychiatrists and sociologists team up to study the excesses of FOMO and its impact on society, they will no doubt devote pages of scholarly research to an enduring ritual that has come to define the beginning of the holiday shopping season. Every year, in the early morning of the fourth Friday of November, millions of Americans take part in the cultural phenomenon that is Black Friday.

Even if you are determined to watch from the sidelines, Black Friday's assault on your Thanksgiving usually goes a little something like this: you're minding your own business, getting ready for a day packed with family, food, and football, when little by little, you come to learn about the deals—the INCREDIBLE DEALS—that are just hours away. There is a clear social media element to the phenomenon, as news of once-in-a-lifetime price reductions spreads virally across the internet. Still, many of the cues that drive Black Friday are steadfastly analog in nature. First, the Thanksgiving edition of your local newspaper is weighed down with shiny flyers that promise spectacular discounts for those intrepid souls who are at the front of the line when the stores open. Then, you turn on the television or radio to be reminded that if you truly love the people in your life, you will prove it by shopping for presents in the dead of night. Finally, in between bites of pumpkin pie, your aunt will announce that she has to get to bed soon so that she can get to the mall by 3:00 a.m. to snag the latest, greatest gaming console for her grandkids, as she does every year.

Apart from the deals—and who doesn't love a great deal—there is plenty *not* to love about Black Friday. Each year, the sales start a little earlier, which means that people who work in retail must upend their holidays, often to work on Thanksgiving itself. Also, Black Friday is no longer an isolated event now that the retail industry has spawned new offspring, including Small Business Saturday and Cyber Monday. Add in Giving Tuesday and the entire week around Thanksgiving has become one massive shopping spree. These annoyances pale, however, when compared to the other tradition that comes along with Black Friday. Every year, without fail, people are injured or even killed when large crowds jostle for primacy in the rush for goods. There's a reason why they call these promotions "doorbusters," after all. Invariably, they bring out the worst in human nature. There's even a site called blackfridaydeathcount.com that documents the casualties caused by stampedes, scuffles, and fights over parking spaces!

When you take a step back, it's clear that Black Friday plays off the same elements that are fundamental to the nature of FOMO: perception and inclusion. First, an asymmetry of information convinces you that you've got to join the masses if you'll have any chance of getting your hands on an amazing deal *while supplies last*. You have no idea what the competition will look like or how many items are in stock, so you've got to be there when the doors open lest you miss out on the savings. Second, the frenzy is designed to tap into the power of the crowd. The entire experience is built on the excitement of racing against your neighbors in the pursuit of the perfect item to put under the tree, next to the menorah, or in your own closet. Retailers pull out all the stops to make sure you'll show up. In 2018, Walmart announced that its stores would throw "parties" to give away four million cups of coffee and two million cookies.[4] These kinds of tactics may sound a little hokey, but they work: approximately 175 million Americans (including me) now shop online or in stores during the weekend between Thanksgiving and Cyber Monday.[5]

Taken together, the forces behind Black Friday amount to a multi-faceted conspiracy to separate you from your family, your bed, and your credit card. It's not the only one. Every day, in ways big and small, you're facing a conspiracy, fueled by a potent combination of biology, culture, and technology, to achieve the same objective as Black Friday: to trigger your FOMO and compel you to make choices that are informed by external factors rather than by your own personal mix of intuition and logic. That's why it's important to remember that you don't choose your FOMO. Rather, it is foisted upon you by a motley crew of players including Apple, Google, Facebook, Snap, every app on your phone, major consumer brands, social media influencers, your cerebral cortex, your ancestors, and the Bible. So, while your FOMO is still yours, as you'll see in the next section, you never really stood a chance.

Why Your FOMO's Not Your Fault #1: Biology

Although the acronym to describe them is new, the impulses behind FOMO are not. From a neurobiological point of view, humans are hardwired to feel FOMO. As far back as *Homo habilis* and *Homo erectus*, our ancestors were hunter-gatherers that lived in tribes and were keenly aware of what they had and what they didn't have but needed in order to live another day. Back then, it paid to be paranoid. If you were wandering around with your fellow hominids and you missed out on a crucial source of food, water, or shelter, all of your lives could be in peril. At the same time, the early humans recognized that another driver of their survival was their continued participation in the very groups that helped them to navigate the harsh environment of the time. If you were cast out of the group or left out of the flow of vital information, you were in danger. You knew that you needed to run in a pack—you needed inclusion—to prevail in the survival of the fittest. Without FOMO, the entire species could have disappeared!

The chemistry that drove our ancestors' FOMO remains present in our DNA even today. Recently, researchers at the University of Michigan published a paper in the journal *Molecular Psychiatry* detailing how the brain has developed a fascinating emotional response to the threat of rejection. The experiment was set up like a nerdy version of a dating app, with subjects sifting through a trove of online dating profiles and ranking those individuals with whom they would be most interested in forming an intimate relationship. Next, the scientists ran brain scans while their subjects learned whether their top romantic interests had reciprocated their overtures or whether they had been rejected. Once all of the tears were dry, the scans revealed that the human brain uses the same natural painkiller system, opioids, to respond to both physical and emotional injuries, such as failure or rejection.[6] It turns out that words do hurt at least as much as sticks and stones, particularly when you're seeking inclusion and acceptance.

It's not only humans that instinctively seek acceptance into a group. Some animal species are hardwired in much the same way. When I observe the migration of Americans to the mall on Black Friday, I am reminded of the wildebeest migration across the Serengeti. Each year, over 1.5 million beasts make a 1,000-kilometer trek from Northern Tanzania into Kenya before turning back and retracing their steps. It's a perilous journey, and some 250,000 animals die along the way, but there is no other option—the wildebeest are instinctually compelled to migrate.

As they make their way north toward the Masai Mara, the wildebeest are packed together, with little space between the tail of one animal and the snout of another, in a line that goes on as far as the eye can see. As the herd advances, the meaning of this seemingly endless parade takes shape. It's a survival strategy based on a phenomenon called *swarm intelligence*. Moving as a herd makes it difficult for enemies to hunt more than a few members at a time, so even when a predator manages to drag off one animal or another, the rest of the group moves forward undaunted. Each animal trusts its instincts because that's how it will survive the long journey across the plains.

You might be asking yourself: What on earth does the wildebeest migration have to do with Black Friday? Everything. If you think about it, they're both examples of herd mentality. FOMO stems from an individual's primitive desire to belong to a group. In that way, we're not so different from the wildebeest. We are driven by our instinct to seek inclusion, which we see as fundamental to our very (emotional) survival. So, when you think about it, all of the people who stampeded in "America's Running of the Bulls" can blame the whole thing on genetics.

That said, there's something important to remember: none of us are wildebeest. If you skip Fyre Fest or your next-door neighbor's *Game of Thrones*-themed anniversary party, there is zero chance that you're going to get attacked by a hyena and die. Unless you live in the Serengeti (where, as any wildebeest will tell you, the probability of that outcome is not statistically insignificant), you can just skip it. Unlike the wildebeest, you don't have to follow the crowd to live another day.

Why Your FOMO's Not Your Fault #2: Culture

The biological roots that have made human beings susceptible to feelings of FOMO throughout history have not gone without notice. As a fundamental part of the human condition, this has been expressed in art, theater, film, religion, and popular culture for millennia.

Consider the Book of Genesis in the Bible. The setting is the dawn of time. Adam and Eve are minding their own business, tending the Garden of Eden, and making sure not to eat from the Tree of Knowledge, as was expressly forbidden by God. Things are going pretty well— they're living in an earthly paradise after all—until the serpent shows up and convinces Eve to eat the fruit of the forbidden tree. He makes her an offer she can't refuse—the fruit is pleasing to the eye, and if she eats it she will know good from evil, just like God. Upon giving in to temptation, she is expelled from the Garden of Eden. For her, that was the price of FOMO.

According to Biblical tradition, Eve was the first person to suffer the consequences of an unwise nutritional decision, but she was most definitely not the last. Whether it's hot peppers, cinnamon, or milk, videos of people ingesting food in all the wrong ways have racked up hundreds of millions of views on YouTube. These stunts are then reenacted in restaurants, homes, and playgrounds, as people all over the world now routinely throw caution to the wind, give in to their FOMO, and participate in inane eating challenges. They are tempted, not by the serpent, but by the chance to join the herd and take part in a meme. Beyond wasting perfectly good food, these antics come with a price. They can land you in the hospital. Five schoolchildren in Ohio who ate the notoriously spicy ghost pepper were hospitalized after suffering allergic reactions.[7] Worse, a man in California spent twenty-three days in the hospital with a ruptured esophagus.[8]

The combination of FOMO and the internet can make people do very reckless things. The same can be said for companies as well. In 2017, Pepsi hoped to capture the imagination of millennials, a prized and politically conscious demographic, via a "short film" called the "Live for Now Moments Anthem." In the film (uh, ad), model Kendall Jenner abandons a photo shoot to join a demonstration that just happens to be marching by. Although it's not at all clear what's being protested (one sign simply says "Love"), Kendall fist-bumps her way to the head of the throng. When she gets there, she strides confidently up to a line of stone-faced riot police. The tension is broken when she pulls out a Pepsi and then hands it to an officer. As he drinks it and smiles, the crowd cheers and hugs in a collective realization that Pepsi just might be the cure for all of the world's problems.

In endeavoring to unite millennials around a love of its beverages, Pepsi managed to achieve something that was perhaps even harder to pull off: it united Americans of all political stripes in the shared belief that its film (uh, ad) was completely tone-deaf. Co-opting images of peaceful protest to sell soft drinks was seen as a trivialization of the very social movements that had inspired the ad in the first place. After widespread backlash, Pepsi pulled the spot in less than forty-eight hours.

It then publicly apologized to consumers and to Ms. Jenner. It was the beginning of a terrible month for Jenner: Fyre Fest took place just a few weeks later.

Whether it's eating forbidden fruit, ingesting forbidden foods, or drinking a forbidden Pepsi, these examples make it clear that FOMO is so embedded in culture that you don't need a smartphone and social media to experience it or pay its price. Before the advent of the internet and social media, newspapers, radio, television, water cooler conversations, and even Uncle Frank's slide show of his cruise to Hawaii all served to stoke feelings of missing out. At the same time, however, in the past twenty years, something has clearly changed. Why, for example, would everyone from *Homo habilis* to Homer Simpson manage to inhabit the earth for millennia without needing a word to describe feelings of FOMO until now? The change, of course, is the emergence of the internet and its transformation of our society from analog to digital.

Why Your FOMO's Not Your Fault #3: Technology

If you want to understand the role of technology in driving modern-day FOMO, think back to the early 2000s, a.k.a. the social media Dark Ages. In the absence of social media, smartphones, texting, and the ubiquitous connectivity ushered in by their combined impact, the world moved differently. Nearly every digital interaction required you to proactively decide to go online. You would power up your computer, connect it to a LAN cable or one of a scarce number of Wi-Fi hot spots, and start surfing or emailing. There were no notifications and no messaging apps to demand your attention every few minutes. In that sense, using the internet was still a lot like watching television. Since you opted in every time you logged on, you controlled the internet, it didn't control you.

Fast forward to the present day. When was the last time you weren't distracted? It was likely the day before you got your first smartphone. Since then, if you had a relatively free moment, like when you were waiting in line or picking up groceries, you probably pulled out your phone. You launched an app, wrote an email, perused social media, played a game, or fired off a bunch of texts. What you didn't do was take a few minutes to daydream or allow yourself to drift off, your mind disengaged and free to roam. Americans now devote over ten hours per day to screen time, much of it on mobile devices.[9] Today, the internet is in charge. It controls you.

What changed? Three powerful forces have fundamentally reordered our relationships with technology and with each other, changing the way we receive information and supercharging the primal instincts that have long made FOMO part of the human psyche. First, we live in an age of relentless access to information. Second, our lives have also been transformed by a surge of extreme interconnectivity ushered in by the rise of social media. Third, all of this information and interconnectivity makes it very easy to compare yourself to other people, whether they live next door or halfway across the globe. The consequence, *reference anxiety*, is especially pernicious in the context of the highly curated world of social media.

1. Relentless Access to Information

Henry David Thoreau famously wrote that "the mass of men leads lives of quiet desperation." Were he alive today, perhaps he'd tweet the following angsty observation:

Henry David Thoreau ✔
@HDThoreau1817

The mass of men lead lives with too much information.

#whyIgotowaldenpond

May 5, 2020

___

We've always lived in a complex and unpredictable world, but until recently, most people were blissfully unaware of what was going on outside of their immediate surroundings. The average person got periodic bits of information from three data sources: television news, print media, and word of mouth. Looking back, it all seems so quaint. Today, the internet delivers a constant stream of live news and hot takes right into the phone in your hands. You can follow anything you want—no matter how niche the story and no matter where you live—in breathless detail. You can also participate, comment, and troll your fellow digital citizens, and in the process, become part of the story yourself.

The massification of digital and mobile communications has drastically shaped how information is received, processed, and disseminated, and the impact of these technologies has been swift. In the ten years from 2008 to 2017, daily time spent consuming digital media in the United States more than doubled from 2.7 hours to 5.9 hours, while mobile media consumption exploded more than 800 percent from less than 20 minutes to over 3 hours per day![10] As a result, access to information has been democratized, it flows from the bottom up, and the sheer volume of data, while exhilarating, is often exhausting and inescapable. But most of all, it's addictive. The Pew Research Center found that 77 percent of Americans go online every day while 26 percent are online almost constantly.[11] In our "always on" society, we have become so reliant on the internet as a source of entertainment, productivity, opportunities, and information that it's nearly impossible to imagine life without it. A recent survey by Asurion found that most Americans believe that they could only survive for one day without their cell phones.[12] To put it in perspective, that's exactly the same amount of time the respondents stated that they could live without food and water.

2. Extreme Interconnectivity

Even as we're drowning in information, our lives have also been transformed by radical connectivity and persistent (over)sharing. The appeal of social media was undeniable from the start. Anyone could be the protagonist of their digital life. Social media started with status updates and the occasional "poke," but soon evolved into a public square where users could share pictures, videos, opinions, or anything else that might elicit a like. Why watch TV when you can create your own drama and get instant feedback in the process?

Surveys have found that 56 percent of people are afraid of missing out on events, news, and important status updates if they are away from social networks.[13] That really means something when you consider that the total number of social media users on earth exceeds 2.6 billion and is projected to surpass three billion, or roughly 40 percent of the globe, by 2021.[14] That suggests that over 1.5 billion people will soon be suffering from FOMO. Given this staggering penetration, whether you are in Palo Alto or Papua New Guinea, you probably spend more than two hours per day tethered to social media.[15] That's more time than most people spend eating, driving, or exercising. Only sleeping, working, and watching TV consume more of our days. It's staggering. In less than twenty years, we have ceded a meaningful share of our lives, *the hours that we*

live in and interact with the world and the people around us, to an entirely
new force.

3. Reference Anxiety

Imagine what would happen if the only tool that anthropologists had to
study humankind was Instagram. What kinds of conclusions would they
draw about modern society? Based on what I see in my feed, I imagine
that they'd marvel at a world inhabited by Brooklyn hipsters who drink
matcha lattes, impossibly cute children who are always smiling, and
people who take pictures of their feet while lounging by swimming
pools. Then they'd probably start to feel slightly inadequate since their
lives couldn't possibly compare.

All of the social media data points you gather online come with
a downside: there is a nearly unavoidable temptation to examine the
lives of others—whether you know them or not—and then assess how
you stack up. People have always compared themselves to their friends
and neighbors. After all, humans are inherently competitive and prone
to insecurity. Yet whereas *Keeping Up with the Joneses* was intrinsically
local, social media makes it frighteningly easy to see snapshots of other
peoples' lives no matter where they live. You can clinically assess their
(online) lives and then judge what your life looks like in comparison. Of
course, you have no idea if these curated images and posts correspond
to reality. Thanks to information asymmetry, you can never quite know
what lies behind the perfect filter.

Who hasn't blocked some of the most conspicuously successful
people in their network from their newsfeed? Hearing about another
person's success and scrolling through their humble brags on a daily basis
gets tiresome, even if you like and respect that person. But no matter how
many people you block, or how much you know that everyone from your

best friend to Selena Gomez curates their digital lives, it's hard to avoid comparing yourself to these unbeatable benchmarks, real or imagined. It's exhausting to keep up with the Joneses—just ask Aloysius McGinis.

At the same time, the grand irony is that you probably can, in fact, keep up, do more, and seek out uncommon experiences with far greater ease than was ever possible before. Prices for flights have fallen by 50 percent in the last thirty years, making it far more affordable and accessible to chase that perfect sunset.[16] Meanwhile, the advent of freelancing, the gig economy, and tech-enabled telecommuting allows for unprecedented flexibility in terms of lifestyle. If all else fails, you can just throw a filter on a snap of your avocado toast, slather on some digital makeup, and convince the world—and perhaps yourself—that you've just posted the greatest avo toast selfie ever.

By doing so, you're taking your first steps in a race to the bottom. When you enter a dishonest battle ruled by digital trickery and asymmetric information, you can never win. No one can. Even if you do "win," your victory is entirely superficial. If you start to measure your self-worth by the number of likes you elicit, you'll soon end up very disappointed. The problem with seeking external affirmation is that it doesn't last for very long. The glow of acceptance will quickly fade, and you will soon find yourself looking for that next rush of validation, just like any other addict looks for their next hit.

If that sounds dramatic, you should know that FOMO is no laughing matter. It carries serious implications for you and for society, so you must remain vigilant. Now that you're aware of the conspiracy to give you FOMO, you're going to start seeing its fingerprints everywhere. You will notice how these external cues drive you to make emotional decisions rather than reasoned ones so that you can no longer trust your intuition. This is the first step to combatting the ongoing daily assault on your senses that comes from seemingly every direction. While some of these intrusions may seem innocuous, taken together, they are far from harmless. As you'll see in the next chapter, even if the factors that turn you into a *FOMO sapiens* look innocent on the surface, the costs that they impose add up surprisingly quickly.

CHAPTER 3

More Than a Meme

"Jealousy is all the fun you think they had."
—ERICA JONG

Over the past several years, a diverse set of brands, from Macy's and Dunkin' to Spotify, have used FOMO or variants of the term in their marketing materials. My favorite, however, has to be the campaign in which McDonald's warned its customers about FOMM, short for Fear of Missing Out on McRib (don't worry, we won't). Meanwhile, Instagram-friendly "art" installations and "museums," with names like Museum of Ice Cream, Color Factory, and Museum of Selfies, have popped up all over the place. My favorite of the genre, The FOMO Factory, set up shop in downtown Austin, Texas, in 2018. For the mere sum of $28, visitors could partake in an "immersive selfie experience," visit a bar that only serves Snapple (one of the exhibit's sponsors), and snap enough pictures to populate their social media feeds for the foreseeable future.[1]

Given its high meme value, FOMO has become a favorite trope of social media influencers, talk show hosts, and hashtag marketers. As such, it's typically regarded as something that's trivial—perhaps even funny—that mostly has to do with selfies and a fear of missing out on parties, vacations, or McRibs. In fact, the top definition on Urban Dictionary (where FOMO made a splash years before it hit the Oxford and Merriam-Webster) supports that perception:

"fear of missing out"

The fear that if you miss a party or event you will miss out on something great. *Even though he was exhausted, John's FOMO got the best of him and he went to the party. #fear#missing#out#party#nightlife*[2]

Unlike the Rickroll, Harambe, Chuck Norris Facts, Tide PODS, and a million other memes that have come and largely gone, FOMO has had incredible staying power. It's now a code word that is widely accepted, especially among millennials. The reason for its privileged perch in pop culture was captured perfectly by *New York Magazine's* The Cut, which wrote, "...terms like 'FOMO' are, generally speaking, a net positive: they help us express something we didn't even know we felt."[3] In that way, FOMO is much more than a meme. It's a condition that affects a large portion of society and that makes people's lives more complicated and less enjoyable. When you finally realize that you're not the only one who is struggling—that there's even a word to describe your feelings—it resonates.

And the struggle is real. *Psychology Today* reports that people with FOMO tend to have lower general mood, reduced self-esteem, and feelings of loneliness and inferiority, especially when they believe that they are less successful than others in their peer group or social circle.[4]

FOMO has also been tied to sub-par academic performance, trouble forming face-to-face relationships, and decreased motivation.[5] Given these implications, this affliction has captured the imagination of psychologists across the world and has compelled them to conduct field-based research to better understand its causes and effects.

Researchers have developed data-driven analyses that show how FOMO directly affects how you see yourself and live your life. For example, a 2018 study of university students revealed that people who have FOMO suffer from "increased fatigue, greater stress, more sleep problems, and physical symptoms."[6] These findings, which were published in the journal *Motivation and Emotion*, also mapped how FOMO varies in relation to an individual's schedule and daily activities. For example, FOMO goes up later in the day and later in the week. It also peaks when you're doing the necessary, but not necessarily fun, things in life, like working or studying. Unsurprisingly, you're at much higher risk to feel FOMO if you're at the library on a Friday night than if you're having lunch with your friends on a Tuesday afternoon. The same study determined that subjects experienced FOMO identically whether they found out about an event digitally or in the physical world, say by word of mouth.

Even if social media serves more as an enabler of these feelings than a catalyst, it plays an outsized role when it comes to provocation. Specifically, it lowers the friction for discovering alternatives to whatever you're doing at the moment. It's a lot easier, not to mention more likely, that you'll find out about the profusion of FOMO-provoking things that are happening around you via social media than by knocking on doors all over campus. Since it serves as a potent accelerant for FOMO, social media is blamed for stress, jealousy, and depression, as well as for causing young people to take undue risks online by posting inappropriate or self-promotional material. It can also spill over into the real world by hurting *offline* relationships.[7]

Whether you get your FOMO from your phone or face-to-face from your friends, there is mounting scientific evidence that you are at risk for real and lasting damage to your life and your livelihood. When the driving motivations behind your decisions are systematically hijacked by your peers, your surroundings, or the internet, you are ceding control, and you no longer have agency when it comes to your own life. While the academic canon devoted to FOMO is expanding, this phenomenon is so new that there is still much to learn and understand about its long-term effects on mental and physical health. As the authors of "Fear of Missing Out: Prevalence, Dynamics, and Consequences of Experiencing FOMO" concluded, "Overall, we believe that social psychology has been missing out on FOMO and call for more research into this phenomenon."[8]

Who says that social psychologists don't have a sense of humor?

It Starts with Generation FOMO, but It Doesn't End There

FOMO is part of human psychology from cradle to grave. If you've ever tried to put a child to bed who wanted to stay up or attempted to get off the phone with your grandparents (who have so many questions!), you already know what I'm talking about. To date, however, most of the attention has focused on millennials. A landmark 2011 study on FOMO conducted by the global advertising firm J. Walter Thompson found that 72 percent of adult millennials can relate to the concept while 41 percent experience FOMO either sometimes or often.[9] While this study was conducted at a time when there was arguably less FOMO than today (apps like Instagram, Snapchat, and Tinder didn't even exist yet!), the implications are clear. This group, which I call Generation FOMO, represents the first wave of true digital natives.

Most millennials never knew a world before the internet, so they've been living online for their entire lives. They have served as the canaries in the coal mine for each new digital product that takes hold in the collective consciousness, from Yik Yak to Tumblr and Vine to TikTok and all of the other sites or apps that their parents never quite understand. They've lived out their awkward teen years, their carefree college years, and basically every other aspect of their lives, online. Almost instinctively, they have become experts at shaping their digital personas for maximum likes, and they'll go out of their way to cultivate the perfect image. While millennials may be getting all the attention (cue the curmudgeons lamenting that once again millennials are making this all about themselves), it's clear that they are not alone. The same J. Walter Thompson study found that over half of Gen Xers and a third of baby boomers can relate to FOMO.

When you remember that FOMO is all about decision-making, things start to make sense. Believe it or not, the first bouts of anxiety begin in early childhood. As you become aware of the world around you and start to sense all of the opportunities that it offers, you also become conscious of the restrictions that are placed upon you and your general lack of agency. You don't decide when to go to bed, you don't get to pick what you eat, and you don't make the rules. That state of suppression lasts throughout childhood and into adolescence, when you get a taste of freedom—although still within boundaries, unless you're a total miscreant. Finally, you reach early adulthood, move out of your parents' house (or not), and start living as you choose.

The independence is intoxicating. It's also overwhelming, especially when you are tempted to compare yourself to all of the new people you are meeting, people from different backgrounds and experiences whose lives can seem quite compelling compared to yours. There is so much to do and so little time, so you try, and fail, to do it all. This "You Only Live Once," or YOLO, infused mindset continues into the post-college years, which in many ways are an extension of college. You are still surrounded by your peers, your herd, which makes for easy comparison and lots of invitations for fun and adventures. This is when it's most tempting to stop thinking for yourself and start making decisions based on all of the external cues that are generated by your surroundings.

A LIFETIME OF FOMO

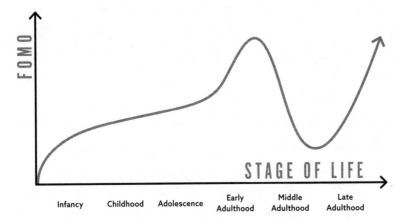

After peaking in early to mid-adulthood, FOMO typically recedes once you reach middle to late adulthood. You're busier than ever both at work and at home, you have less time to think about what you're missing, and you're tired. Staying out all night has real consequences the next day. Plus, the information asymmetry that enables FOMO is not as powerful as it once was. You've had a lot of experiences in your life, so when new opportunities cross your plate, you already have a sense of what you will be missing. That makes it so much easier to go ahead, pick what makes the most sense for you, and just miss out. You can breathe a sigh of relief. The struggle is over. Or is it?

Even when you think you've got it licked, FOMO can make a strong resurgence during the later stages of life. First, there is the risk of a mid-life crisis. After all of those years with your head down, you finally look up and realize that you now have more years behind you than you have left. The stereotypical dash to buy too-tight jeans and a flashy sports car says it all. Then, once you retire, you have far more free time to fill. You're also more aware of your mortality and the fact that you won't be able to do all of the things you want to do forever. Your set of choices is only going to diminish from here. If you dream of making that once-in-a-lifetime trip to India or taking the grandchildren to Disneyland, you'd better do it now while you've still got your health. Although it's no fun to think about, you know that at some point, you will once again find yourself following rules set by others, just as you did as a child. Someone, your adult child or caretaker, will take over the logistics and you will no longer be in control. It's now or never!

Are You a *FOMO Sapiens*?

Now that you understand how FOMO manifests itself, you also know that unless you live in a remote cave, it's nearly impossible to avoid the factors, both online and in the real world, that trigger it. Your only option is to learn to manage it. One way to start this process is to be honest about how FOMO is changing your behavior and shaping your decisions. You can begin to appreciate where things stand by taking a diagnostic test that was created by a team of psychologists and published in the academic journal *Computers in Human Behavior* in 2013. This series of questions, which has been cited frequently in the research community, has also made the jump to internet culture. It has been shared widely online and, ironically, I suspect that its ubiquity comes down to FOMO. If you find out that your friends took the test, you don't want to miss out on the opportunity to do the same.

As you answer the questions below, it's interesting to note that only one item makes explicit mention of the internet. These questions identify behaviors that are universal. Still, it's easy, or even tempting, to give in to these latent anxieties in the digital age. All you have to do is pick up your phone, and you've unwittingly opened the door to activating and even supercharging them.

Self-Assessment Questions

For each of the ten questions below, rate yourself on a scale of 1 (not at all true of me) to 5 (extremely true of me).

1. I fear others have more rewarding experiences than me.
2. I fear my friends have more rewarding experiences than me.
3. I get worried when I find out my friends are having fun without me.
4. I get anxious when I don't know what my friends are up to.
5. It is important that I understand my friends' in-jokes.
6. Sometimes, I wonder if I spend too much time keeping up with what is going on.
7. It bothers me when I miss an opportunity to meet up with friends.
8. When I have a good time, it is important for me to share the details online (e.g., updating status)
9. When I miss out on a planned get-together, it bothers me.

10. When I go on vacation, I continue to keep tabs on what my friends are doing.[10]

Next, find the average score for your responses across all ten questions.

OK, now that the results are in, what do they tell you? Before drawing any hard conclusions, it helps to remember to keep things in perspective. Even if you score an average of 5 across the entire assessment, this is an indicative measure, not a formal evaluation by a licensed therapist. Rather than seeing your score as a final verdict, think of it as a way to take the pulse of where things stand. Now that we've cleared that up, you can interpret your score. In their research, the authors surveyed a sample of 2,000 users aged 22–65 and found that the average result was approximately 2.[11] Thus, if you score below 3, you're pretty average. It's once you get above 3 that you join the ranks of the *FOMO sapiens*. If that's the case, don't worry. You will learn how to change that in the final two sections of the book.

It's encouraging to know that you can take control of the decisions that you make and, in doing so, neutralize FOMO. But fixing FOMO on its own won't necessarily solve your problems. After all, it's no longer the only FO in town. There is another FO, FOBO, or Fear of a Better Option, that also drives your choices (or lack thereof), both personal and professional, on a daily basis. Yet unlike FOMO, FOBO has largely stayed behind the scenes, lying in wait for just the right moment to make a name for itself. I find that surprising since I've always believed that FOBO is just as relevant, or even more so, than FOMO. I've also learned that, as two sides of the same coin, they must be tackled together since they have many of the same root causes. As you'll see in the next chapter, while the power of FOMO is strong, there is most definitely another FO you need to know.

CHAPTER 4

The Other FO You Need to Know

"The best is the enemy of the good."
—ITALIAN PROVERB

Have you ever spent an inordinate amount of time struggling to decide between two perfectly good options? Or perhaps you committed to a social or professional opportunity only to bail at the last minute? Maybe you invited someone to an event via text only to notice they started to formulate a response and then stopped, erased it, and disappeared? You know that they were writing you back, you saw those three pensive dots, but then…radio silence. If so, then you're already acquainted with FOBO.

While FOMO drives you to try to do absolutely everything, FOBO is quite the opposite—it induces paralysis. FOBO is a mindset in which you always strive to choose "the best" when you're faced with a decision. As you search for the perfect alternative, you also keep all of your options open. This makes it unattractive—or even impossible—to commit to any of the alternatives in front of you, so you live in a world of equivocation rather than one of yes or no. Living this way is not easy. You spend precious time and energy poring over all of your possible choices only to procrastinate well past the point when you should have decided and moved on to something else. While constantly kicking the can down the road can feel good, even comfortable in the moment, the costs add up quickly. FOBO is time-consuming, exhausting, and inefficient. If left unchecked, this behavior can cause irreversible damage to your career and, more broadly, your life.

It can also impact the lives of others. When you have FOBO, you are a burden to all of the people around you who are waiting for you to commit to something—anything—so that everyone can move on with their day. Until you do so, the people who are awaiting your decision cannot plan the vacation, the business trip, the meeting, the deadline, the date, the negotiation strategy, or the wedding. They can never truly believe that you are "all in" on anything. The minute that something better comes along, you will change your mind, send your regrets, and either bail or make a halfhearted effort at keeping your word. In the most extreme cases, you simply ghost people. No matter how you send the message, you are neither invested nor committed.

For this reason, FOBO is far more toxic than FOMO. FOMO doesn't make you a rotten person, but FOBO does. FOBO makes you say *maybe* instead of committing, go silent when it's time to finalize plans, and cancel at the last minute when something better comes along. Whereas FOMO only hurts the sufferer, FOBO impacts everyone around the afflicted. And of the two FOs, FOBO also tends to be a much longer-term problem. It's an affliction of affluence that typically intensifies as you get older, more established, and wealthier, all of which tend to give you more choices in life. That's when it transcends bailing on coffee or dinner and permeates every aspect of personal and business relationships. The more possibilities that you have at your disposal, the more overwhelming your set of choices, the greater the temptation to preserve option value, regardless of whether you waste the time or hurt the feelings of others. You are also less likely to care how your behavior affects other people. You've got options, after all.

The Biggest Problem You Didn't Know You Had

More often than not, when I explain FOBO to someone who has never heard of it, I get the same reaction. Their eyebrows shoot up, and they point a finger at their chest exclaiming, "That's me!" Sound familiar? Although you might never have heard of FOBO before you purchased this book, there's a pretty good chance that you or somebody close to you is already living with it. But without a word to embody this behavior, it's been difficult to call it out.

All of that changes starting now. It's time to name and shame FOBO. It's also time to give it a proper definition since I've never done so in the past. When I first wrote about it back in business school, I knew that in addition to being total *FOMO sapiens,* my peers were such *FOBO sapiens* that they required no explanation. The same vast set of opportunities that drove a culture of FOMO also made it surprisingly difficult to choose decisively from the array of possibilities. Since most of my classmates and I had worked for a few years and saved money, we could pretty much do as we pleased, assuming that we could get out of our own way and commit to something.

Absent a proper definition, until very recently, FOBO was not only anonymous, it was also somewhat amorphous. All that changed in the summer of 2018 when Tim Herrera of the Smarter Living section of the *New York Times* defined it in his column:

> It's the relentless researching of all possible options for fear that you'll miss out on the "best" one, leading to indecision, regret, and even lower levels of happiness.[1]

While I like Herrera's take, I'm going to take it one step further with a comprehensive definition that will frame the discussion going forward:

FOBO

\'fō-(,)bō\ Noun. Informal

1. An anxiety-driven urge to hold out for something better based on the perception that a more favorable alternative or choice might exist. **2.** A compulsion to preserve option value that delays decision-making or postpones it indefinitely. **3.** Behavior that turns you into an entitled a**hole.

As you can see, FOBO is characterized by two distinct yet powerful impulses:

→ First, it's grounded in a belief that there is at least one better option out there waiting to be discovered. If you're *holding out for something better*, then you will keep searching until you find it, taking great pains to avoid making any decisions in the meantime.

➡ Second, it's a mindset in which *preserving option value* carries just as much importance as making a selection. By keeping all of your options open, you believe that you can dictate the decision-making process on your own terms.

When you combine these two behaviors—holding out for something better and preserving option value—you'll find that it's nearly impossible to commit to anything, at least on a timeline that others will find acceptable. This sense of entitlement, that the world must work on your schedule and cater to your needs, creates a toxic environment that has the potential to alienate all of the people who are beholden to your whims. Basically, it makes you an a**hole.

Holding Out for Something Better

When you have FOBO, you are convinced that there must be a better alternative out there, even if it has not yet presented itself. Of course, when you are operating in a choice-rich environment, it is not unreasonable to assume that there is something better out there and that you can *optimize* your outcome if you resist the urge to settle. The abiding belief that something better just *has* to be out there might seem like a form of optimism, albeit one that is fueled by information asymmetry. A pessimist, with his glass half empty, would assume that things can only go downhill from here. It takes an optimist to believe that better and brighter days—and options—lay ahead. While such a mindset would usually be seen as a positive approach to living life, when it compels you to embark on an endless search for alternatives, it is rooted in risk aversion.

Although such overoptimization is harmful, that's not to say that you must blindly accept the first thing you're offered. If the soup is cold, if the hotel room is drafty, or if the salary offer is stingy, don't suffer in silence. You can ask for what you want and negotiate for something better if the situation requires. Doing so doesn't mean that you're suffering from FOBO, it means that you know the value of your time or your money. Your behavior crosses the threshold if you keep searching based on the unreasonable expectation that you will unearth something so compelling that your decision will instantly seem straightforward and your downside will be zero. While that sounds nice in theory, there is no way to know if a decision is ideal, either in the moment or long after the fact. Absent perfect information, such a calculation will always be somewhat subjective. But if you have FOBO, you reject that notion. Your biggest fear and the factor that drives your thinking is that you will end up with second best, so you prefer to keep searching while you run down the clock. In doing so, you have walked straight into a trap that will mire you in indecision.

Preserving Option Value

You have FOBO when you prize option value, in and of itself, to the point that you are paralyzed. You live by a cardinal rule: never close any doors or eliminate any potential options. Whether you're making weekend plans, looking for a life partner, or searching for a job, you will be reluctant to eliminate anything from the stack. Even as you continue to add new items to the pile of possibilities, you take solace in knowing that if you change your mind at any point, you haven't closed any doors. Your decision-making process isn't exclusively focused on finding the best, it's also fixated on maintaining maximum flexibility. Otherwise, you run the risk of ending up worse off than you could have been. You will regret the road not taken and be miserable. Your life will be, gulp, sub-optimal.

Your response to this fear is to keep all of your options open, discard none, and procrastinate. In a sense, you are a hoarder. Yet instead of hoarding cats or shoes or those back issues of *The New Yorker* that you're going to read someday, you are hoarding possibilities. That way, you'll never have to worry about waking up one day and wishing that you had said yes to that ski trip or that you had invested in that real estate project. The people who are waiting for your response may get sick and tired of catering to you, but if they decide to move on without you, that's on them, not you. As long as you don't say no, you'll have zero regrets. You can still get everything you want and deserve. You can still live happily ever after. In this way, indecision itself becomes the final bulwark that protects you from doing the wrong thing.

If you believe that you can control the timing of your decisions, you also believe that you have leverage. It's easy to start to believe that you are the master of your own destiny. Unfortunately, that's a delusion. While you may get away with FOBO some of the time, it will eventually catch up with you. The more you delay your decisions, the more you run the risk that a number of your potential alternatives will simply fade away. As deadlines approach and perhaps pass, the world may very well move on without you. You will quickly lose control and find out the hard way that you are no longer in the driver's seat. You've got to act—and quickly!—if you're going to avert disaster. At this point, ironically, your mindset shifts. Rather than optimizing or hoping for the best of all options, you instead shift into risk-mitigation mode. You'll take what you can get, hoping for *something, anything,* rather than ending up with nothing at all.

In the next chapter, we will explore the forces that make it tempting—or even irresistible—to hold out for something better. As you'll see, factors such as psychology, technology, and good old-fashioned narcissism combine to breathe oxygen into FOBO. Part of what makes this mix so potent is that it doesn't necessarily look too dangerous on the surface. On the contrary, the desire to have more choice and to pick what's absolutely best for you seems logical. But as you'll see, that doesn't always result in autonomy. For someone with FOBO, it's far more likely to be a prison.

CHAPTER 5

The Sad Tale of the Man Who Got Everything He Wanted

"It is easy to get everything you want, provided you first learn to do without the things you cannot get."
—**ELBERT HUBBARD**

When it came to watching movies as a kid, I didn't suffer from a lot of FOBO. Without Netflix, Amazon Prime, and all of the other services that offer limitless selection today, I made do with whatever was on HBO, FOBO be damned. That's why I've seen *Willy Wonka & the Chocolate Factory* more times than I can count. Even though I haven't seen it in years, I can still recite the last three lines of the film from memory. Just after Mr. Wonka gives his chocolate factory to young Charlie Bucket, as they surge upward into the cosmos in Wonka's storied glass elevator, they have the following exchange:

Mr. Wonka: "Don't forget what happened to the man who suddenly got everything he wanted."

Charlie Bucket: "What happened?"

Mr. Wonka: "He lived happily ever after."

Leaving aside the obvious corporate governance issues that arise from handing over a complex manufacturing facility to an adolescent, I've always been affected by that ending, which in its sentiment is as gooey and sweet as anything coming out of Wonka's factory. With age, I've also come to understand that the notion that you can get everything you want is the emotional equivalent of Wonka's confectionary legacy: the Everlasting Gobstopper. Sure, it's cool, tastes great, and promises to last forever, but it's got limited nutritional value and will eventually rot your teeth.

The myth that you can have it all is built on the very big assumption that you actually know what you want and are capable of choosing it. That's the hard part. Even if, like Charlie, you can have exactly what you thought you wanted all along, will you live happily ever after? Who says Charlie even wants to run a chocolate factory? When Wonka hands him the keys to the business, Charlie's got no other real options—he's so poor that all four of his grandparents are living out their final days from the same bed. He'd be crazy not to go for it.

At this point, it's instructive to consider a counterfactual. What if Charlie already had lots of other possibilities beyond becoming a chocolate magnate when Wonka offered him the factory? If he had been considering attending college in another city, backpacking through Asia, or playing lead guitar for a rock band, how might his reaction have changed? Would he still live happily ever after?

If he saw his future through the eyes of Sylvia Plath, the answer is no. Rather than basking in a world of endless possibilities, she only sees

peril as options multiply. In this passage from *The Bell Jar*, the proliferation of choice is so paralyzing that she ends up with nothing at all:

> I saw my life branching out before me like the green fig tree in the
> story. From the tip of every branch, like a fat purple fig, a won-
> derful future beckoned and winked... One fig was a husband
> and a happy home and children, and another fig was a famous
> poet and another fig was a brilliant professor, and another fig
> was Ee Gee, the amazing editor, and another fig was Europe and
> Africa and South America, and another fig was Constantin and
> Socrates and Attila and a pack of other lovers with queer names
> and offbeat professions, and another fig was an Olympic lady
> crew champion, and beyond and above these figs were many
> more figs I couldn't quite make out. I saw myself sitting in the
> crotch of this fig tree, starving to death, just because I couldn't
> make up my mind which of the figs I would choose. I wanted
> each and every one of them, but choosing one meant losing
> all the rest, and, as I sat there, unable to decide, the figs began
> to wrinkle and go black, and, one by one, they plopped to the
> ground at my feet.[1]

Plath's stark vision of a fig tree encircled by its own rotting fruit
represents the polar opposite of the escapism of Willy Wonka. It's also
far more relatable to anyone who has struggled to make sense of the
many distinct pathways that life offers to each of us. Even if you are fortunate to have amazing opportunities all around you, part of the challenge
that comes with making choices is that you must simultaneously let go
of what you cannot choose. Although I'm sure someone has pulled it off,
most people cannot have a happy family life, take a bunch of lovers with

strange names, travel around the world, and be an Olympic champion all at the same time. In order to pick your lane, you have to make trade-offs and turn down all of those other exotic, exciting, and wildly different adventures. But which path should you choose? How do you know which way is the right way? If you don't know what you want (and most people don't), choosing one course of action and forgetting the rest can be daunting. It feels risky.

To break the logjam, it seems rather self-evident that you must learn to come up with criteria that will enable you to choose from among the various alternatives at your disposal. Intuitively, the point of setting the criteria should be pretty obvious: you want to choose *the best*. At a minimum, you want the best from the range of possibilities that are available to you. That's not particularly controversial, is it? You certainly wouldn't aim to choose the worst, and why should you settle for something in the middle?

As it turns out, the answer to that question is not as straightforward as it might seem. As with FOMO, biological factors play a central role in driving FOBO as well. The very human desire to want the best, when combined with narcissism and the explosion of choice for nearly everything your heart could desire, can become your own personal fig tree. The combined effects of these three factors can make navigating through life feel surprisingly overwhelming, even when it comes to the small things you encounter on a daily basis.

The Biology of Wanting the Best

There is nothing inherently wrong with wanting to have choices or with seeking out the best possible alternative. If ambitious people don't aspire to make the most of themselves and the world in which they live, the pace of progress will grind to a halt. It's necessary. It's also hardwired into the human psyche. Those very same hunter-gatherers who feared exclusion from their prehistoric herd were also instinctually compelled to maximize their resources. To achieve this objective, they were highly mobile, choosing to pack up camp and set up again in a new location once foraging for food became too difficult and time-consuming. This behavior is nature's equivalent of time equals money.

When you're a hunter-gatherer or a bee looking for pollen, the criteria for deciding whether you should maximize your opportunities by heading somewhere else are pretty straightforward. Since you know what you need in order to survive and thrive, you can objectively determine whether your current environment is sufficient. If it isn't, your decision is made for you. Your only other alternative is to innovate, start planting crops, and build a food source that no longer requires you to be a nomad. That is your choice, and it may determine whether you live or die (no pressure).

Just as choice is critical to survival, it also makes life better and more appealing. How boring would it be if you only had one choice when it came to the things you use every day? With more options, you can better align the things that you consume with your actual wants and needs and, in doing so, make more of your time and money. Through your choices, you can express yourself and select your own path to fulfillment. Problems arise, however, when you consider how an ever-expanding set of variables makes it harder and more time consuming to determine which option is actually the best.

In the now classic book *The Paradox of Choice*, psychologist Barry Schwartz makes the case that having more choices makes settling on just one of them far more stressful and difficult. Crucially, he looks at how this dynamic affects *maximizers*, or people who "seek and accept only the best."[2] If you're a maximizer, you evaluate as many alternatives as possible to ensure that you have achieved your objective. In doing so, you invest much more time and energy than your peers studying the various alternatives before trying to whittle them down to a winner. This stands in stark contrast to the behavior of a *satisficer*, or a person who chooses to "settle for something that is good enough and not worry about the possibility that there might be something better."[3]

Ironically, or as Schwartz would say, paradoxically, even though you are likely to make better choices when you're a maximizer, you will ultimately be less happy with those choices. That's because as a highly selective person—i.e., someone with FOBO—you've evaluated so many potential alternatives that you're stressed out and prone to risk aversion lest you suffer buyer's remorse. It's highly ironic when you think about it. You've done your homework and made a better decision. You chose a better house, spouse, car, or hotel than the satisficer down the street, but you cannot properly enjoy the fruits of your labor. Even though you got everything you wanted like Charlie Bucket, you will not live happily ever after.

Maximization isn't just tied to biology, it's also got a strong cultural component that is shaped by your upbringing, national origin, and social class. If you're American and grew up in the middle class, for example, you've likely been groomed from a young age to believe that freedom and autonomy, in the form of choosing to do whatever you want to do, is fundamental to your basic right to "Life, Liberty, and the pursuit of Happiness" as was set out in the Declaration of Independence. You've been taught that in America, freedom of expression and choice is part of the social contract. It's what allows entrepreneurs to chase after crazy dreams, convinces children that they can be anything they want when they grow up, and liberates artists to challenge the status quo with their work. For all of these reasons and many more, the value of choice likely seems self-evident to you, as it does to me.

But is it? Working together with Schwartz, Hazel Rose Markus of Stanford University found that perceptions of choice vary widely depending on culture and social class.[4] For example, while North American society lionizes individualism and sees choice as an essential cultural norm, in other more collectivist societies, such as those of East and South Asia, there is far greater emphasis placed on interdependence and the impact that your decisions and actions will have on other people. Moreover, working-class Americans tend to teach their children that the world does not revolve around them and that you must follow the rules and conform to the system if you want to get ahead. So, while affluent parents in brownstone Brooklyn are telling little Poppy or Jack that the world is their oyster, the working-class family next door in Queens or on the other side of the world in Bangladesh is imparting a very different set of messages to their offspring.

If you've grown up believing that you can shape your own destiny, that you have autonomy, and that an abundance of choice equates to freedom, you may also take the fact that you have the ability to choose for granted. But choice, like many vital resources, is not spread evenly across the world. It is this abundance or scarcity of selection that fundamentally shapes decision-making.

The Commodification of Choice

For much of human history, people were so preoccupied with securing the basics in life—things like food, clothing, and shelter that are found at the lower levels of Maslow's hierarchy of basic needs—that they didn't have time for high-class problems like FOBO. Today, things have gotten a lot more complicated. Where *Homo habilis* had to get a few really important decisions right, modern humans, particularly those who live in affluent societies, face a much more complicated set of calculations on matters large and small. If you find Barry Schwartz's work on choice and satisfaction as compelling as I do, it's incredible to think that *The Paradox of Choice* was published way back in 2004 at around the same time that my friends and I were first calling each other out for letting FOBO interfere with our lives. Looking back, our struggles seem so quaint. That was before the iPhone, social media, texting, and perhaps the greatest choice-enabler of them all, Amazon Prime. Basically, it was the Stone Age of choice. Over the last fifteen years, all of these new technologies and services have made it far easier than ever before to be a maximizer and to succumb to the temptation of FOBO.

Today, you probably have many more options than the most privileged members of society just a century ago. Depending on where you live, you don't need to be particularly rich or well-connected to recognize that you have an abundance of choice when it comes to most anything you could care to consume on a daily basis. Choice has become a commodity, and as it's gone mass market, it's had clear implications for the beneficiaries of all of these new alternatives. It can be overwhelming. In a very real sense, you are spoiled for choice, and if you cannot manage that dynamic, you will repeatedly fall into the trap of indecision.

As you know, you cannot have FOBO if you don't have choices. A glut of choices, often fueled by affluence, is a fundamental element of the affliction. On the other hand, if you don't expect additional options to come your way, then your problem is over before it even begins. Imagine you're waiting for an organ transplant, and you're fortunate to receive the call that a donor has been located. If you find yourself in this position, you don't ask the doctor if there might be a better organ available next week. You don't hold out for someone a little younger, a little fitter, or who never had a drink of alcohol in her life. On the contrary, you grab your things, get in the car, and count your blessings all the way to the hospital. That's your *only* option, one that lots of other people are literally dying to have for themselves, so you take what you can get, and you're grateful for it.

Compare that with a typical Saturday morning at your local Starbucks. First of all, there's nothing life and death about the situation, even for the biggest caffeine addict. Second, there is an insane amount of choice available for a product that costs just a few dollars and takes less than five minutes to prepare. That's how Starbucks ended up being the place where someone sidles up to the barista and proclaims that today they'll be having a Venti, iced, half-caff, ristretto, four-pump, sugar-free soy Skinny Cinnamon Dolce Latte. Thanks to orders like that, Starbucks prides itself on offering more than 80,000 different drink combinations.

The abundance of drink options at Starbucks is not an isolated development. It is emblematic of how a choice-rich environment makes even the most innocuous decisions unnecessarily complicated. Thanks to advances in manufacturing, the shift away from physical goods to digital goods, and the rapid pace of globalization, businesses are able to offer many more products, often tailored to your specific wants and needs, than they did in the past. They can also provide an array of choices to consumers that would have seemed fantastical just twenty years ago. Fast-fashion retailers like ZARA or H&M now translate an idea from the runway to their global network of stores in as little as two weeks. Amazon can offer 10,000 times the selection of your local supermarket, not to mention that it never closes, it tailors pricing to the individual consumer, and it allows you to instantly enjoy millions of books, songs, and movies from the comfort of your sofa.

This should be a good thing, right? Shouldn't all of your FOBO be solved if someone hands you exactly what you want? While the exponential growth of choice and customization looks like a panacea on the surface, it's actually quite the opposite. If you want the world served up in a way that is specifically tailored to your wants, needs, and likes, you still have to *know* what you want, need, and like in order to pull the trigger and say yes.

Who Says There's No Me in FOBO?

Keeping your options open for as long as possible is a prerequisite to having FOBO, but this impulse is supercharged when your desire for control is rooted in naked self-interest. Everyone has that friend, family member, or coworker who never quite commits to anything. It's the guy who returns everything he buys weeks or months later because he changed his mind. When you run into him at a party, he's always looking over your shoulder in hopes of finding someone better to engage in conversation. He never accepts the first table he is offered at a restaurant or the first room he is assigned at a hotel. He wants to check out a few rooms or take a look across the dining room first so that he can assess the relative pros and cons. Warning: if you're going to have dinner with him, make sure to sit at the other end of the table. Since he couldn't bear to choose just one thing from the menu, he's going to ask everyone around him if he can try their dishes too.

Someone with FOBO doesn't see this sort of activity as a problem. "What do you mean," he'll protest in shock, "why should I settle for second best?" True, there is nothing wrong with having standards, but there's a big difference between setting basic criteria and optimizing each deliberation to the point that you lose perspective, complicate routine decisions, and make life way more complex than it needs to be. *When you approach life as if it were a negotiation in which the goal posts are constantly shifting, it is nearly impossible for others to meet you in the middle.* Since there is no middle, you end up inconveniencing everyone around you, and your interactions become increasingly transactional in nature. By trying to have your cake and eat it too, you are never willing to make a trade-off. Instead, you expect everyone else to make the concessions.

On your quest for perfection, you are crippling yourself with a major character flaw: narcissism. In a June 2017 op-ed titled "The Golden Age of Bailing," *New York Times* columnist David Brooks captured the nation's attention for at least a few hours—pretty impressive in the age of FOMO—by describing how FOBO has permeated relationships:

> It's clear we're living in a golden age of bailing. All across America people are deciding on Monday that it would be really fantastic to go grab a drink with X on Thursday. But then when Thursday actually rolls around they realize it would actually be more fantastic to go home, flop on the bed and watch Carpool Karaoke videos. So, they send the bailing text or email: "So sorry! I'm gonna have to flake on drinks tonight. Overwhelmed. My grandmother just got bubonic plague...."[5]

Here's how you know that your behavior is driven by narcissism. When you bail on your former colleague, are you doing it for her? Do you think to yourself, "I just want to give her a break for one night— she'd be much better off binge-watching something on Netflix than seeing me"? No way! People with FOBO commit to a range of social and professional opportunities, but they're never actually fully locked in until the moment they step into the room at the appointed hour. At any time prior to that, whether it be a day or an hour beforehand, they mentally reserve the right to bail. They send a text or an email with an excuse, either real or imagined, and move on to the best available option for that moment in their life. Inherent in their narcissism is a simple calculation: their time is more valuable than yours.

Technology has a clear role to play in this cycle of broken commitments and ghosting. In the analog past, say more than fifteen years ago, if you wanted to cancel on someone or change plans, you had to call them on the phone and talk to them. There was no way you would get a text halfway through the evening that would convince you to bail and do something else. Today, you can avail yourself of multiple low-friction ways to break plans, even when you are in the middle of them. Plus, you can hide behind technology, which makes the experience relatively painless. While you may feel "bad," you don't have to deal with the consequences beyond a few electronic exchanges back and forth.

The intersection of narcissism and FOBO happens when your compulsive desire to keep your options open becomes a defining characteristic of the way you live your life. Everyone needs to change plans once in a while or impose on others in one way or another. But when you string multiple people along before responding to simple questions, consistently keep your assistant late to compile fifty different agendas for your trip, or make your analyst work every weekend running endless—and arguably pointless—changes to the pitch deck, you have FOBO, and everyone around you is paying the price. This is not behavior that is restricted to high-level executives in Wall Street boardrooms. It's found among employees at all levels of a wide range of organizations, whether they're working at a small business in Germany, a tech start-up in Nairobi, or a corporate sales department in Miami. It's everywhere.

A Lifetime of FOBO

For many people, some level of FOBO is inevitable. No matter where you live or what you do, at some point, complexity inevitably creeps into your life. When you mature from childhood to adulthood, you must learn to live with a daunting increase in the number of decisions you have to make. Making more decisions has obvious positive effects. You get to decide where you're going to live, what you're going to do for a living, what time you want to go to bed, and what you're going to drink (red, rosé, or white?) at dinner. While you have far more autonomy than ever before, it's not all wine and rosés. You must make choices that are boring, difficult, or just no fun. That's when you realize that when you were a kid, you had it pretty good. I'd much rather spend a few minutes choosing one item from a pile of toys than waste half my weekend evaluating insurance plans.

During infancy and childhood, the fact that you live in a highly controlled environment where you don't make many choices makes it pretty difficult to have FOBO. Even if you're a notoriously picky eater, your parents will only be able to accommodate you so much until they give up and decide to starve you out of your funk. If you tell them that you don't want to eat fish sticks, they're not going to pass you the iPad and let you order from any restaurant you want. They're going to let you sit with your fish sticks until you decide to eat them or, if they're feeling particularly magnanimous, they'll give you chicken fingers instead. They're in control.

As you reach adolescence, life starts changing quickly. You acquire a modicum of independence, and your base of experiences grows, allowing you to begin calibrating your likes and dislikes. You may also start dating, which unleashes a wave of unfamiliar emotions and possibilities. As you enter adulthood, your propensity to have FOBO will be directly correlated with how choice-rich life becomes. If you finish high school and take over the family business or work at one of the two companies in your hometown, there's not much to feel FOBO about, at least on the professional front. You're settling into a pretty clear path, one that you're familiar with since many people around you have chosen something similar. On the other hand, if you move to a new city to enroll in college, flirt with a half dozen majors, interview with a broad range of companies, and surround yourself with people who are doing the same, the outcomes of your choices are wildly unpredictable. In such a choice-rich environment, your risk for FOBO is infinitely higher.

From there onward, the more success and wealth you accumulate, the more likely it is that FOBO will increasingly factor into your life and shape your approach to living it. Even as you get busier and have less time to spend on important decisions, you will also have the resources to consider a greater number of potential options. You will also start to place a higher value on your time. If things have gone well for you, your appraisal of your worth is going to be a lot higher than it was ten or twenty years ago. At this point, risk aversion and narcissism also take on a larger role in driving behavior. You fear making the wrong choice and wasting your precious time and energy on something that won't make you happy. After all, you say to yourself, you deserve it. You work hard, you're busy, and your time is valuable. Your wants and needs, and those of your family or inner circle, must be your only concern, even if your actions and attitude cause collateral damage to everyone else who is affected by your decisions or lack thereof.

If you continue on the same path, one of relative affluence and an abundance of choices, your FOBO will continue unabated until you reach a juncture in late adulthood when your outlook on the world starts to change. At that point, the power that FOBO holds over you begins to recede. You've accumulated a lot of life experience and you've chipped away at the information asymmetry that clouds so many of your decisions. Most importantly, you know that time is of the essence. Every moment you spend agonizing means less time to enjoy the fruits of your labor. Drawing upon the wisdom you have accumulated over a lifetime, you recognize that the best option of all is to make sure that you don't waste another precious minute on FOBO.

FOBO IN A CHOICE-RICH ENVIRONMENT

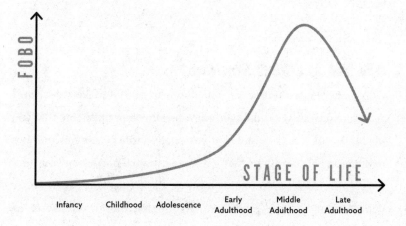

The progression of FOBO over a lifetime, as shown on the previous page, is an archetype for someone who is operating in a choice-rich environment. No two lives unfold in the same way, of course, and so there are two important caveats to bear in mind. First, the ebbs and flows of FOBO, particularly the curveballs you encounter, will determine whether you follow this progression or end up tracing one that is radically different. If things don't go as planned—you lose your job, separate from your partner, or face some unforeseen calamity—you may find that life is unrecognizable. You will no longer live in a choice-rich environment, at least when it comes to that very important aspect of your existence. Second, the use of the term choice-rich does not necessarily correlate directly with economic wealth. Although it often does, your lifestyle and your social environment will also determine how you perceive the scope of possible opportunities within your grasp. There is no reason to assume that the Fortune 500 CEO who goes to Davos every year will be any more fulfilled than the Buddhist monk who has never left his village. In fact, the opposite may very well be true.

Are You a *FOBO Sapiens*?

Do you have a reputation as someone who cannot make a decision? Are you constantly rescheduling or canceling commitments that you made days or weeks before? Do you spend more than a few minutes deliberating about things that will have minimal impact on your life? If you answered yes to one or more of these questions, then you're definitely on the FOBO spectrum. In order to know for sure, however, you've got to think a little deeper about how you make decisions and how your methodology (or lack thereof) affects you and everyone around you. The questions in the following diagnostic test all highlight behaviors and attitudes that are present in people who exhibit chronic FOBO.

In order to determine if you're a *FOBO sapiens*, you will need to gather the answers to two distinct sets of questions. First, you will complete a self-assessment, just as you did to determine if you were a *FOMO sapiens*. Next, you will answer the second set of questions by posing them to the people in your inner circle. One of the defining characteristics of FOBO is that it directly affects those in your orbit, so your family and friends will have both the knowledge and the incentive to answer honestly and accurately. If you're deluding yourself or just don't realize how your behavior is affecting others, this will serve as a wake-up call to help you to see where you stand.

Answer each of the following questions on a scale of 1 (not at all true) to 5 (extremely true).

Self-Assessment Questions

1. I spend an inordinate amount of time or energy making relatively unimportant decisions (i.e., things I won't remember in a week).

2. I do not feel I can make a good decision unless I have numerous options to weigh. Even if I have an acceptable choice in hand, I seek to generate other alternatives before committing.

3. I often make multiple reservations, appointments, or sets of plans and wait until the last minute to choose one (or none) of my options.

4. I often reject the first thing I'm offered (such as a table at a restaurant, a hotel room, or the purchase price of an item) and try to negotiate or trade up to something better.

5. I frequently purchase items that I end up returning later on.

6. I see canceling on commitments, even at the last minute, as an unavoidable by-product of my busy life.

7. I have damaged personal or professional relationships due to my inability to commit to plans or other decisions.

Questions to Ask Others

8. Do I struggle to make decisions and to commit to one course of action?

9. Do you see me as a "flake" or as someone who is unreliable?

10. Do you avoid making plans or decisions with me due to my inability to commit?

Next, find the average score for the responses to all ten questions. If your average score exceeds 3, then you can count yourself among the ranks of *FOBO sapiens*. If you averaged more than 4, then I'm amazed that you're still here given all of the other options you have at the moment! All joking aside, the list of tendencies compiled in this assessment is certainly not exhaustive. You likely know someone (and depending on your score, *are* someone) who lives under the yoke of FOBO. If you're wondering why someone who acts in a way that is so often selfish could possibly be described as "living under the yoke" of anything, consider this: beyond the costs and sacrifices that you impose on others, you are also paying dearly for a set of behaviors that seem, on the surface, to offer you freedom. By placing option value first, you fail to realize that rather than lifting the weight of the decision-making process by…making a decision, you remain trapped in the inhospitable no man's land that lies between ambiguity and certainty. Subconsciously, or perhaps even consciously, in the occasional moment of clarity, you recognize that you're in a terrible bind—you'll never actually be happy, or at least move on, until you make a decision. But you cannot. You are stuck in purgatory.

THE HIDDEN COST OF FEAR

"The difference between successful people and really successful people is that really successful people say no to almost everything."

—WARREN BUFFETT

CHAPTER 6

The Billion-Dollar Business of FOMO

"It's only when the tide goes out that you learn who's been swimming naked."

—WARREN BUFFETT

In 2018, NPR's *Marketplace* ran a report titled "FOMO in China is a $7 billion industry."[1] The protagonist of the piece, a young father named Chen Jun, lived in a small apartment in Shanghai along with his wife, his daughter, his parents, and his brother's family. Although he had a stable job, he was impatient and was in search of a plan to improve life for his family. Then one day, everything changed when he stumbled upon a podcast called "The Path to Financial Freedom." For just $29 per year, he could learn how to trade cryptocurrencies directly from Li Xiaolai, China's richest bitcoin mogul. Emboldened, he quit his job in order to trade cryptocurrencies full-time. What could go wrong? Everyone else was making a fortune buying and selling bitcoin, so why not him?

It turns out that Chen is not alone. China's "pay-for-knowledge" economy is powered by consumers who are desperate to upgrade their skills in hopes of staying relevant in a very competitive labor market. Their fear of falling behind the pack is so palpable that a Chinese think tank publicly attributed the size of the knowledge industry to FOMO.[2] Purchasing courses assuages these fears and, for Chen, opened a door to a new career. He didn't stop there. He became an avid consumer of pay-for-knowledge products and even subscribed to a podcast called "How to Make Your Voice More Attractive."

What stood out to me about Chen Jun's story wasn't his prodigious appetite for risk or his equally voracious appetite for podcasts. Rather, I was struck by the fact that Chen was awash in several different types of FOMO at the same time. Not only had FOMO convinced him to invest a meaningful amount of his cash flow into self-improvement, but it also compelled him to bet his family's financial future on speculative investments in bitcoin—all based on a get-rich-quick scheme he heard about on a podcast! Worse, as of the date that the *Marketplace* report was filed in September 2018, bitcoin had fallen almost 70 percent from its peak of nearly $20,000.

I don't know where he is today, but I genuinely fear for what has become of Chen, his cryptocurrency investments, and his sprawling family. Although bitcoin had basically crashed at the time of the report, it went on to fall another 50 percent over the next three months. While it has gone on to recover some ground and might even reach $20,000 again someday, investing in any kind of speculative asset can devastate a small investor, especially one with limited experience. No podcast can protect you from losing a lot of money when you don't know what you're doing. Ironically, just two weeks after the story ran, Chen's inspiration, Li Xiaolai, announced via the social messaging app Weibo that he would no longer be investing his money in blockchain, the basic technology that enables cryptocurrencies.[3] He decided it was time to make a career change. I sincerely hope that Chen followed his lead.

How FOMO Drives Commerce

When FOMO is applied to commerce, it is used to achieve a singular goal: to entice you to do something that you wouldn't do, or would delay doing, without external stimuli. FOMO may be a multibillion-dollar business in China, but based on that criteria, I'd hazard to guess that the market easily reaches into the hundreds of billions of dollars across the globe. The FOMO-related surge in bitcoin's value alone topped US$200 billion in 2017.[4]

In order to understand how FOMO influences business, it's helpful to once again deconstruct it into the two basic components— *perception* and *inclusion*—that were laid out back in chapter 2. Each of these elements is responsible for one of the two types of FOMO— Aspirational FOMO and Herd FOMO—that drive marketing and commerce:

➡ **The Role of Perception in Aspirational FOMO:** When you trust in perception, your actions are predicated on a belief that your decisions will make your life better than it is at the moment. Given this desire to improve your standing, this can be referred to as *Aspirational FOMO.* Of course, you must also suspend logic to an extent: given that information asymmetry can cloud your judgment, it's impossible to know whether reality will live up to expectations.

➡ **The Role of Inclusion in Herd FOMO:** Seeking inclusion is centered on an instinctual desire to make sure that you are not left behind. It's your brain reminding you that emotional rejection will elicit the same neurological response as physical pain, so you'd better make sure that you don't let that happen. In honor of the mighty wildebeest, which is also instinctually compelled to stick with the crowd, this can be called *Herd FOMO*.

Aspirational FOMO

From Serena Williams and Jake Paul to Huda Kattan and Cameron Dallas, influencers drive billions of dollars of commerce each year by promoting products to their followers. In essence, they are selling a dream—an aspiration that is *bigger, better, and brighter* than the drudgery of the real world—based on the *social proof* generated by their fame. Social proof is the idea that people will look to influencers in society when making decisions in their own lives. It is the engine that powers Aspirational FOMO and the fundamental reason that celebrity endorsements exist in the first place. It's no coincidence that *AdWeek* projects that influencer marketing will be a $10 billion market by 2020.[5]

While social-proof-driven commerce is big business, monetizing your followers by selling or promoting things for cash is nothing new. Famous people have been peddling random stuff you didn't know you needed for years—just ask George Foreman. What has changed since the rise of social media is not the *presence* of influencers—it's the way we follow them. George Foreman showed up in a few infomercials, but that was the extent of the sales process. Thanks to social media, influencers now have a direct line into our phones and our psyches through which they can feed us intimate snapshots of their lives. By posting photos or videos from their homes or their vacations, they tell us about their families, their fears, and their favorite things. They are the trendsetters in an online culture that has increasingly become tethered to attention-seeking in the pursuit of affirmation. As a result, they expose their dark sides (and sometimes their backsides) through Twitter meltdowns (Miley Ray Cyrus, over 40 million followers), Instagram feuds (Justin Bieber and Selena Gomez, combined over 250 million followers and counting), or ill-advised bouts of revenge porn (Rob Kardashian, banned, at least for now, from Instagram).

This attention-seeking, however contrived, has the effect of making these individuals seem far more real and infinitely more human than they would if their airbrushed image were plastered on the cover of a glossy magazine. By convincing us that they are #authentic, influencers can more effectively promote products, events, or other commercial ventures. If they're truly good at what they do, they can drive your FOMO without you even realizing that you're being manipulated. Since you care about these people, their ups, their downs, their kids, their feuds, their trips to rehab, and their dogs, you are invested in them. That's what makes it possible for them to make the sale in the first place.

Always remember, however, that *they are not invested in you.* Consider the Instagram accounts of Cristiano Ronaldo, Selena Gomez, and Ariana Grande, who were the most followed celebrities in 2018. Taken together, this group has amassed more than 500 million followers, yet they collectively follow fewer than 2,000 people themselves. You may be following them, but they definitely aren't following you. The relationship is fundamentally one-sided. That's the weird thing about social media: you actively choose to be a *follower* and to consume the content of lots of people, from celebrities to your next-door neighbors. As a result, content from people you know well and who are actually part of your life is juxtaposed with content from people who have no idea that you even exist.

When you look at it that way, influencer-follower relationships are far more fraught than they appear on the surface. Mixed in with baby pictures and photos from your cousin's wedding are hidden advertisements from your influencer "friends." Thanks to information asymmetry, you have no idea if the influencer actually believes in the product he is pitching or if he's just collecting a paycheck. Given the amount of money at stake, there is a good chance that he's using you, although he'll never say that to your face. The ugly part of the business is kept well behind the scenes. Once in a while, however, the truth comes out. In *Fyre*, the Netflix documentary about the Fyre Fest saga, the cameras capture the harsh reality that drives the most cynical of influencer-centric marketing schemes. Sitting on a beach in the Bahamas flanked by Ja Rule and some of the Fyre Starter supermodels, McFarland explained they were "selling a pipe dream to your average loser. Your average guy in middle America." *Ouch.*

Herd FOMO

Retailers and marketers design entire campaigns that are predicated on provoking your FOMO so that you will decide to spend money on the goods, services, and experiences they are peddling. From the stampedes of Black Friday to the days-long lines outside of the Apple store in hopes of snagging the new iWhatever, the purchasing process has long been an integral part of the overall experience for some products. Just like the wildebeest, the compulsion to participate is motivated by a fundamental need. For the wildebeest, it is survival, and for the *FOMO sapiens,* it is acceptance and inclusion. The comradery of taking part in something bigger than yourself—the anticipation, the planning, the shared experience, and the stories that will be told for weeks or years after—becomes another core benefit of the product. In that way, it's ego expressive. It

The Herd in Two of Its Natural Habitats: Africa and the Apple Store

tells the rest of the world who you are and how you fit it. It's also a visual cue to everyone who happens to pass by that they too should join in.

That's why chef Dominique Ansel directs his team to bake less than 400 Cronuts (a mashup of a donut and a croissant) to sell each morning from his bakery in Manhattan's SoHo neighborhood. If you want to get your hands on one, you must famously line up well before the bakery opens its doors at 8:00 a.m. While Ansel could make more of the product or raise its price to match demand, he knows that the hysteria surrounding the Cronut—a word that he has trademarked—is worth far more than maximizing daily sales. First, the limited daily offering creates *scarcity value*. Second, those long lines outside the bakery prove that what he's cooking up is truly worth the wait. Unlike the social proof provided by celebrities or influencers, however, this social proof is derived from the strength of the herd, in the form of all of the cranky New Yorkers and giddy tourists who are standing in line. When done right, the combination of these two ingredients makes for a recipe with Cronut-level potential.

For Ansel and his bakery, all of this FOMO means valuable PR, the kind of exposure that money cannot buy, in the form of crowdsourced

Facebook posts, tweets, and 'grams. However, it says a lot about herd mentality that one morning in 2016 while the store was deluged with consumers #dyingforacronut, the line extended past a man who had died some hours earlier on a bench. It is one thing to be enraptured with that perfect selfie or post, but it is quite another to be so enmeshed in the herd that you lose sight of people in the real world who might need your help.

While clever tactics like Ansel's have long been a powerful motivator to build brands and sell goods, over the last decade, online marketers have figured out how to translate the same combustible mix of Herd FOMO, social proof, and scarcity to the digital world. Digital marketers use all kinds of tools to get your attention and to try to make you decide that you just *have* to have their product. Once you realize the tricks they use, it's sort of like seeing *The Matrix*. You'll never browse the web the same way again.

Imagine you decide to take a vacation in Las Vegas, a city that knows a lot about how to market FOMO. You head over to the American Airlines website and after a few clicks, you're served up an array of flights. As you browse, you notice it says "three seats left" under your preferred option. Knowing that it's now or never, you lock it down. On the next page, you're presented with a "limited-time offer" to sign up for a credit card that offers a bonus of $250 along with lots of free miles. You skip the credit card but on the next page—surprise!—you get one more crack at signing up for that same "limited-time offer." You escape once again only to learn that seats are running low, so you'd better seize the moment if you don't want to get stuck in the middle row by the bathroom. You agree to pay forty-five bucks and then—surprise, again!—you get a third chance to sign up for that credit card via the "limited-time offer." Finally, you are enticed to purchase trip insurance via a notification that over

93,000 travelers just like you opted for such coverage in the last seven days. By my count, that's at least six instances of social proof and scarcity value standing between you and your seat.

Whether you are operating in the digital or the physical world, it's undeniable that both Aspirational FOMO and Herd FOMO are deeply woven into how marketers of all stripes fight for attention and sales. If you stay attuned to these messages, whether overt or subliminal, you will learn to wrest back control and make decisions that correspond with what you *actually* want rather than what you *think* you want as a result of their efforts. Changing that power dynamic is critical not only to making choices that genuinely reflect your preferences, but also to making sure that you do not suspend your judgment as you do so. Not only will that help you to avoid eating too many Cronuts, but it will keep you from risking your money on speculative investments.

Fear (of Missing Out) and Greed in Silicon Valley

Asset bubbles typically start and end the same way. Before prices rise beyond the point of reason, a combination of true believers and smart investors pile in and start driving up both the price and the public profile of an investment. All of a sudden, making money looks easy. You start to think that if you don't move soon, you'll miss the chance to get rich quick. As prices rise and become irrational, the only way a bubble can sustain momentum is to appeal to investors who don't demand a connection to reality to jump into the fray. These new investors are compelled by Aspirational FOMO and greed, both of which trump rigor and reason. These are the people who buy bitcoin after they hear about it from their nephew during Thanksgiving dinner, the people who buy gold after seeing a commercial on their favorite news channel, or someone like Chen Jun who decides to jump headfirst into a speculative market based on a podcast. Watch out, the herd has arrived.

Once Herd FOMO sets in, conventional wisdom dictates that the "smart money," namely, experienced investors who are subject-matter experts, cash out. As they run for the hills, their pockets stuffed with cash, they leave the market to the herd. Finally, when the bubble bursts, cooler heads prevail, and the market returns to earth. Those investors who fall victim to FOMO—those who bought late and speculatively—are left to pick up the pieces. If only they had looked at the myriad cases of similar bubbles over the course of history—from the stock market crash of 1929 to the Beanie Babies bubble of the 1990s—and figured out that they were the ones being played. All they had to do was spend a few minutes Googling "FOMO and bitcoin." If you try it, you get more than 900,000 results.

In the rarified air of Silicon Valley, the conventional wisdom about smart money doesn't always hold. In fact, the smart money can end up looking pretty stupid. Take the case of Theranos, the now-defunct Silicon Valley darling that claimed it had the technology to test for hundreds of illnesses with just a drop of blood. Unlike bitcoin, this is a debacle where the bubble was fueled by a group of "sophisticated investors" who should have known better. The company managed to raise a staggering $700 million of funding from high-profile investors like the media mogul Rupert Murdoch, the DeVos family (the owners of Amway), and the Waltons (of Walmart). In the process, they drove the company's valuation to a princely sum of $9 billion. It's safe to say that none of these investors could claim it was their first time at the rodeo, but it made no difference. All of them were wiped out when the company's founder, Elizabeth Holmes, and her partner, Ramesh "Sunny" Balwani, were charged with "massive fraud" by the SEC.

How did Holmes pull off such a spectacular rags-to-riches-to-rags tale? She used the same tried and true tricks as Fyre Fest and Dominique Ansel with his Cronuts. First, she stoked Aspirational FOMO by using social proof to create an air of inevitability about the company's eventual success. When her idea was still a PowerPoint deck, she secured an early investment from Tim Draper, her former neighbor, who also happens to be one of the most prolific figures in the Valley. As the company grew, she doubled down on social proof by recruiting former U.S. cabinet secretaries and senators to the Theranos board of directors. For outsiders considering making an investment or inking a strategic partnership with the company, it was clear that a lot of smart people thought that they were going to make boatloads of money.

That's where Herd FOMO came into the picture. Rich and powerful people talk, and although none of these esteemed figures had any scientific expertise, they helped to pull other powerful people into the fray, both as investors and evangelists. Once she had the herd circling, Holmes used scarcity to get prospective investors to wire their money with minimal information. She was also careful to avoid skilled investors with domain expertise, such as respected venture capital firms whose partners were industry experts and would not invest without conducting thorough due diligence. If you asked too many questions about the company's "highly proprietary" technology, you were out. In addition to its success in raising cash, Theranos managed to secure transformational partnerships with companies like Safeway and Walgreens by playing to their FOMO: both companies were desperate to lock down an exclusive partnership that would make their leadership teams look like heroes. Shockingly, they installed the technology in their stores without proof that it actually worked!

At some point, Holmes's plan worked so perfectly that it created a self-reinforcing cycle. She used her investors and board to attract new partners like CVS and Safeway and then leveraged those partnerships to attract even more money, talent, and buzz to the company. This very powerful herd had taken on a life of its own. Holmes had everyone fooled, and for one shining moment she was included in the Forbes 400 list of the richest Americans. Then, the cracks started showing, the technology failed, and at long last, the people in the herd started asking questions. They realized they had been duped. When Holmes's downfall began, it was swift. In just a year, her net worth nose-dived from $4.5 billion to basically nothing![6] That had to be awkward.

While the Theranos fiasco is unprecedented in many aspects, the outsized role that FOMO played in the company's trajectory is not. Although a fear of missing out is most certainly not a compelling reason to make an investment, it can convert the otherwise rational men and women who chase after start-ups for a living into a rowdy herd of *FOMO sapiens*. I get it. In my own career as a venture capitalist, either investing my own capital or working for VC firms, FOMO has at times snuck into the rationale for an investment. I once invested in a start-up led by a former Latin rock star who behaved like he was in an altered state the entire time we worked together. I wish I could have missed out on that one—the investment went bust in record time. *Every time I've allowed FOMO to supersede logic, I've lost money.* I learned the hard way that FOMO causes you to invest in industries you don't understand with people you don't know. It convinces you to outsource your judgment to the herd—especially if that herd is full of reputable people—rather than doing your own homework. It's a recipe for disaster.

You Can't Defy Gravity Forever

Even if you remain impervious to FOMO, you will face critics. Suppose that as a sensible and judicious investor, you say "no thank you" when you get the chance to invest. Although you may say "no thanks" to an opportunity for all the right reasons, watching your friends hit it big while you sit on the sidelines can be gut-wrenching and can invite lots of criticism, especially from everyone in the herd. Back in 1999, *Barron's* published a piece titled "What's Wrong, Warren" that chastised Warren Buffett for failing to pile into the internet bubble. The article, which I have to think *Barron's* would now love to bury in a very deep hole, went on to suggest that Buffett was too old-fashioned, "conservative, even passé" because as a 70-year-old, he didn't "get" the tech sector.[7] Ageism aside, the article accused Buffett, the Oracle of Omaha, of missing out by only investing in sectors he understood. They were right, he did miss out…when the Nasdaq eventually fell 87 percent over the next several years. As Buffett shows, in order to succeed in the long run, you should stick to your knitting and invest based on analysis and not emotion.

While your rigor will help you to eventually be proven right, like Buffett, or to avoid investing in companies like Theranos, at other times, you just get it wrong. You turn down a professional opportunity that ends up being spectacular…for someone else. Nothing good can come from counting someone else's money—money that could have been yours! If you're going to escape the temptation to feel jealous or wracked with regret, you're going to need to reframe the way you see the situation. No matter how much success you've had in the past, it's essential to remember that you cannot defy gravity. As a result, part of overcoming FOMO is accepting the fact that sometimes you will miss out on rewarding opportunities. That's easier said than done, which is why you've got to respect a VC firm like Bessemer Venture Partners. In addition to listing successful investments like Staples and LinkedIn on its website, Bessemer prominently highlights its "anti-portfolio" as well. The anti-portfolio is a list of companies where the firm had the chance to invest but didn't. For example, when it came to Google:

> David Cowan's college friend rented her garage to Sergey and Larry for their first year. In 1999 and 2000 she tried to introduce Cowan to "these two really smart Stanford students writing a search engine." Students? A new search engine? In the most important moment ever for Bessemer's anti-portfolio, Cowan asked her, "How can I get out of this house without going anywhere near your garage?"[8]

Google wasn't the firm's only big miss. What happened with Facebook might be even more painful in hindsight, considering that Friendster, a primordial social network that was hot in the early 2000s, was largely irrelevant by the end of the decade:

> Jeremy Levine spent a weekend at a corporate retreat in the summer of 2004 dodging persistent Harvard undergrad Eduardo Saverin's rabid pitch. Finally, cornered in a lunch line, Jeremy delivered some sage advice: "Kid, haven't you heard of Friendster? Move on. It's over!"[9]

By highlighting these missed opportunities and counting the foregone millions (or perhaps billions), Bessemer does a lot more than show that it has a sense of humor and a healthy dose of humility. It also signals that it accepts that even the smartest investors cannot and will not be able to spot every opportunity. In fact, in order to dedicate sufficient time and resources to the small group of companies in which the firm does invest, it is going to have to focus, act decisively, and say no *a lot*. The more efficiently it does so, the better, although it's inevitable that amazing opportunities will slip through the cracks due to misjudgment or circumstance. By accepting that harsh reality and even celebrating it, Bessemer removes the fear from its culture and replaces it with common sense. Ironically, the firm's move toward transparency has been so well received that the anti-portfolio has now become a standard fixture on many other VC firms' websites. By jumping into the anti-portfolio herd, I'd argue that these copycat firms might have beaten one kind of FOMO, but they have replaced it with another.

A FOMO-driven strategy has implications beyond making investment decisions in the gilded bubble of Silicon Valley. It can also cause leaders to question their convictions and companies to lose their way. As with speculative bubbles, technological change also affects how companies operate and position themselves in the market. Seemingly overnight, historically dominant players face upstarts, once innovative ideas seem stale, and panic and uncertainty rule where stability once reigned. It's at these moments that companies can find themselves suffering from FOMO. In order to find their path forward, they look around and try to keep up in any way that they can. They seek to defy gravity, but they too end up crashing back to earth. That's why Amazon launched its failed Amazon Fire Phone, Pepsi developed Crystal Pepsi, and Long Island Iced Tea changed its name to Long Blockchain Corp. and stated its intention to reinvent itself as a cryptocurrency player. The Fire Phone and Crystal Pepsi failed long ago and were pulled from the market. When Long Island Iced Tea's stock price shot up nearly 300 percent, dozens more companies, from poker machine markers to juice companies, joined the herd and tried to pivot to blockchain. It didn't work. One year later,

Long Island Blockchain traded 97 percent lower than during its bitcoin moment, and it was delisted from the Nasdaq. As the shareholders of the world's first iced tea/blockchain company learned the hard way, FOMO is *not* an investment strategy.

CHAPTER 7

FOBO, the Anti-Strategy

"As long as you don't choose, anything remains possible."
—MR. NOBODY

If your parents read you fairy tales when you were a kid, you are bound to have heard the classic story of a young blonde girl who commits a brazen home invasion. It's called "Goldilocks and the Three Bears." But just in case you grew up in a Goldilocks-free household, let me fill you in. It's about a young girl who happens upon a cabin in the woods. Although nobody answers the door, she decides to drop in and make herself at home.

Once she gets inside, Goldilocks finds three bowls of porridge on the table. The first one, it turns out, is too hot, while the second is too cold. The third is just right, so she helps herself. She then fusses between three chairs, which she judges too hard, too soft, and just right. Finally, having tired herself out with all of that FOBO, she ends up sleeping in the most comfortable of the three beds. In the course of one afternoon, Goldilocks certainly left her mark. She ate all of

the porridge, broke a chair, and
made a mess of the bedroom.
When the resident bears return
home, they are understandably
angry, so they chase her off, and
she's never heard from again.

Revisiting this story as an
adult, I see two clear takeaways.
First, blondes really do have
more fun. Second, Goldilocks's

FOBO—fed by narcissism, a plethora of choices, and an unwillingness to
settle—has made her a total jerk and a criminal. With each of the decisions
she made that day in the cabin, she put her short-term desires and objectives above those of the innocent family of bears that would be impacted
by her actions. She's entirely transactional, and that kind of behavior has
consequences. While doing what was best for her felt good at the time,
and was apparently also exhausting, she paid the price in the end.

If only the harshness of FOBO were strictly the stuff of fairy tales.
If you want to see it in the real world, just download the dating app
Tinder, which was designed from the outset to exploit the desire for
option value. If you've never used Tinder, here's how it works: The app
presents an endless stream of potential romantic matches based on
your location. Each time a new profile picture comes up, you can either
swipe right if you want to chat with the person or swipe left if you're not
feeling it. The entire process takes two seconds, so if you've got reasonable finger dexterity you can scroll through dozens of potential matches
every few minutes.

When you're carrying a singles bar in your pocket, you can spend
hours rejecting potential dates until you find someone you deem worthy

of a rightward swipe. You don't have to commit, heck, you don't even have to talk to anyone, you can just sit in your underwear and swipe away. Isn't it romantic? Now take that approach to dating and apply it to everything in your life: your career, your friendships, your relationships, and your business. If you were to treat the people with whom you work—whether they are colleagues, suppliers, or clients—like the people in your Tinder feed, you would most certainly cause lasting damage to your career.

Consider the case of a friend of mine I'll call Alex. Alex hated his job and was desperate to get another one in the same industry. He was also very keen to move from New York to somewhere in Europe. His top choice was Paris since he had family there, but he was willing to go almost anywhere on the continent. He just wanted out of his current job. After months of interviews, he finally managed to get an offer from a firm in London. He loved the job; in fact, it met all of his criteria, except that it wasn't in Paris. He asked himself, "Should I swipe right or swipe left?"

That night, Alex embarked on a last-ditch effort to convert his new offer into a better option on the other side of the English Channel. Just before bed, in a fit of FOBO, he sent an email to a friend in Paris asking for advice on how to leverage the offer he now had in hand for something equivalent in Paris. It was only when he woke up the next morning and opened his email that he realized his mistake. He sat up in terror. He hadn't emailed the friend as intended—he had emailed the very person in London, his future boss, who had made him the offer the day before. The response he received was short and far from sweet: "You have twenty-four hours to accept our offer or consider it withdrawn."

Alex had been caught red-handed, but he was also incredibly lucky. Lots of employers would have rescinded the offer on the spot. Why would a company want to be someone's backup plan? Facing the ultimatum that sat in his inbox, he realized that his FOBO had gotten the best of him. He had risked a very good, nearly ideal option that he would have gladly accepted when he first started his job search. In doing so, he'd been reckless. Alex accepted the job in London without daring to ask for any of the improvements that he would have contemplated in a normal salary negotiation. When he started his new position, he wondered whether his actions would cost him anything at his new firm—he was effectively already on probation before he even started. He'll never know the answer.

How FOBO Is Remaking the Labor Market

Of course, being someone's backup isn't limited to job interviews; it can gradually come to permeate every aspect of how you map your professional trajectory until it becomes the defining characteristic of your career. In a 2018 survey, LinkedIn reported that 68 percent of workers feel FOBO when making career decisions, while 17 percent say their biggest professional regret is not holding out to get their "dream job." In a blog post announcing these findings, the company described how FOBO plays out in the workplace:

> Picture this—you were just offered a new position at work, or even a new job. Initially, you're thrilled by the opportunity, but then thoughts of possible better options flood your mind. "Is this the right fit for me? What if I could find a role that offers more pay, a different title, more flexibility, the option to work from home?" Now you are struggling to make any decision. You are experiencing FOBO—the fear of better options—and you're not alone.[1]

LinkedIn may look like a social network on the surface, but it has created an entire business model out of giving people FOBO when it comes to their careers. That's because it's a major hub for job searches, with nearly 80 percent of recruiters using the site to fill positions.[2] Every time you log in, you are bombarded with job listings, messages from head hunters, and status updates that tell you all about the career moves and promotions that are happening within your network. While some of those features are clearly designed to give you FOMO, they are also like catnip for your FOBO. LinkedIn is becoming Tinder for jobs, and if you're unhappy in your career or determined to make a change, you can spend hours looking for something better. It also provokes a lot of angst, which does nothing to help you find the elusive job of your dreams.

FOBO's effects on the job market go far beyond the four corners of the LinkedIn app. It's also one of the main drivers behind the gig economy, the rising tide that has made freelancing a career path. The gig economy has spawned an entire generation of digital nomads who work from anywhere and jump from one project to another without committing to a set path. The effects of this shift on the U.S. labor force are stunning: over 40 percent of Americans are expected to be freelancers by 2020.[3] Of course, not all of these people are full-time freelancers, so this figure requires a bit of unpacking. Some of these workers are using their gigs to supplement income at full-time jobs or to generate income during unemployment. Still, plenty of others, millions of people, have opted to hang out a shingle and go into business for themselves. Often this takes the form of a portfolio career whereby an individual strings together a bunch of different activities that, collectively, constitute her "job." If you want to see this phenomenon in action, just walk around a coworking space like WeWork or any coffee shop in the world and ask people what they do all day.

The freelancing revolution is a product of three secular trends. First, it's powered by the internet, which makes all of these flexible work arrangements possible. Second, it is a direct result of the end of lifetime employment, as once prestigious and predictable pathways in industries like law and finance have disappeared, pushing many professionals out of firm life and into consulting roles. Finally, lots of large companies are shifting to a freelancer-centric labor model in order to fill gaps on their teams, drive productivity, and access talent without having to offer standard benefits packages.

While building a portfolio career can provide some clear benefits in the form of flexibility, autonomy, and a paycheck, doing so can also be a wolf in sheep's clothing that stokes FOBO. You'll never have to commit to one project, you'll always have as much option value as you could want, and you'll be free, unencumbered by the shackles that weigh down all those working stiffs in the corporate world. You are a *free*lancer, in every sense of the world, but that freedom can come with a cost. Flexibility is also inherently unpredictable, and you must constantly hustle to lock down that next project if you ever hope to have predictability with respect to your future earnings. You are also unlikely to ever participate in the value that you create for your clients. You can design the most amazing logo, write some epic lines of code, or come up with a brilliant marketing strategy, but the rewards will stop at your paycheck. You won't participate in the upside that comes with a promotion, a raise, owning stock, or any of the myriad incentives that businesses use to provide long-term compensation to their employees. Option value is nice, but it will not make a down payment on your apartment or put gas in your car.

How to Lose Friends and Not Influence People

The relationship between FOBO and your career does not flow in only one direction. While FOBO may shape how you do your job, your job can also very much dictate how you feel FOBO. If you're successful, the experiences and rewards that flow from your profession, and the choice-rich environment that they create, can eventually catch up to you. The irony is that FOBO-fueled behavior is completely acceptable in many industries. Being the ultimate holdout can be seen as a very tough and effective negotiating tactic in professions like law and finance. If you know how to use it as a weapon, you can move up the ranks and pad your pockets with all of the money it makes for you. This is where things get particularly dangerous. The more you deploy FOBO at work, the more comfortable you feel doing so in all other aspects of your life. Behavior that would have once seemed selfish, unkind, or even silly becomes increasingly common and comfortable. It all becomes a vicious cycle. Your personal FOBO feeds your professional FOBO, which only increases your personal FOBO, and on and on.

All of that is somewhat sustainable when things are going well and you have leverage. But if lots of your options disappear overnight—maybe you lose that high-powered job or your company merges or goes out of business—you start to see the world from the other side of the FOBO power balance. It's hard to be a narcissist when you've gone from hero to zero, and you find yourself at the center of a big, cosmic, "I told you so." At these moments, simple truths become clear: no matter how well you do in life, there will always be times when you need to rely upon the kindness of others. If you haven't earned that kindness, or if you have squandered it, don't expect it to be there when you need it most.

When FOBO becomes much more than a negotiating strategy, when it becomes a life strategy, it can contaminate your relationships, with some serious long-term effects. While you are holding out on decisions and expecting the world to accommodate you, the people around you start to notice. Maybe not at first. At first, your friends and professional contacts are probably willing to tolerate your behavior. "He's a super busy guy," they think, or, "She's got a lot on her plate," they say, giving you the benefit of the doubt. They give you a free pass, one you don't deserve, but hey, who's keeping score. After the next time, and the next time, and the next time, however, something changes. They finally see your behavior for what it is.

In this way, FOBO is like a long con. You can do as you wish for a time, but at some point, those around you figure out what you're doing. Eventually, the people who have been tolerating your FOBO will note your selfishness and see its effects on them. Unless they have zero self-regard or have no power, they will not let you treat them like that anymore. That's what causes a loyal employee to jump to a competitor, a trusted partner to set out on her own, or a faithful supplier or client to sever a relationship. Destroying relationships is just the first in a series of negative effects that can result from FOBO. The toll that this behavior can take goes well beyond relationships and can contaminate the strategic decisions of organizations of all sizes.

Indecision, Inc.

Even as FOBO infects your personality and changes your behavior, it will also directly and negatively impact how you run the day-to-day aspects of organizations both large and small, whether they are entrepreneurial ventures, corporations, or government entities. It is the ultimate productivity killer and the polar opposite of having a winning strategy. It's actually an anti-strategy in that it does the opposite of all of the things that a good strategy should achieve. It destroys your momentum and limits your effectiveness by (i) breeding analysis paralysis, (ii) stifling innovation by preserving the status quo, and (iii) surrendering leadership to inertia. It can also combine with FOMO to compound indecision and stasis.

Falling into the Quagmire of Analysis Paralysis

Making decisions, even day-to-day, business-as-usual decisions, is hard work. You must trust your homework and accept that you cannot predict the future. If you are unwilling to face disappointment, regret, the inevitable trade-offs, or even failure, it's more appealing to avoid deciding altogether. As you seek ways to eliminate unknowns or generate additional options, you eventually wade into the territory of analysis paralysis. FOBO, when it manifests itself in such a way, creates a culture of waiting for the next report, the next milestone, or the next board meeting, before taking action. In some ways, however, FOBO and analysis paralysis can pass themselves off as sensible behavior. Who would fault you for doing your homework, running tons of scenarios, and generating as many options as possible before plotting a path forward? Only later, when you've missed an opportunity or fallen behind, will it become apparent that you moved too slowly.

Take the case of Audi, one of the leading car companies in the world, with over €65 billion in sales.[4] Its annual R&D budget exceeds €4.5 billion, which makes sense for a company whose slogan, *Vorsprung durch Technik*, means "Advancement through Technology."[5] Yet despite its engineering prowess, installed base of loyal customers, and financial resources, Audi has struggled to keep up with its peers in the race to bring an electric car to the market. One automotive journalist noted the magnitude of what ended up being a slow-motion car crash:

While other car companies (most notably Nissan) made a firm decision to make and sell an electric car three or four years ago—and now sells EVs by the thousands—Audi continues to study the issue. At the…Los Angeles Auto Show, running through Nov. 27, Audi is now showing its all-electric A3 e-tron—what it calls a "technology study."[6]

Unfortunately for Audi's executive team, that assessment now seems charitable: the quote taken above is from 2011. Yes, you read that correctly. Despite debuting a first-generation electric concept car at the 2009 Frankfurt Motor Show, the company's executives failed to commit to a design, a production schedule, and a marketing plan. Now, a decade later, the company is nowhere to be found in the fight for the future of the automobile industry. As a result, the price of indecision is adding up, with the foregone profits and growth easily reaching into the billions of dollars. So much for *Vorsprung durch Technik*.

Audi's misadventures are a textbook case of FOBO. The company spent an inordinate amount of time, money, and resources trying to figure out exactly how it was going to design and launch a product. It studied the market, produced concept cars, and spun its wheels—both literally and figuratively—for years even as upstarts like Tesla and established players like GM and Nissan ate its lunch. When and if it does eventually commercialize its technology, the stakes will be astronomical.

Analysis paralysis is particularly dangerous with the advent of "big data." Thanks to the asymptotic decline in the cost of storing information, as well as the growing sophistication of data science, the market for big data has now surpassed $200 billion.[7] In fact, more data has been created in the last two years than in the history of the human race.[8] While these new tools offer tangible advancements for decision-makers, they also make their jobs more complicated: the bigger the haystack, the harder it is to find the needle. As this trend accelerates, companies will be tempted—or even expected—to collect ever greater amounts of data. They will also seek to dedicate more resources to quantifying all possible risks before moving forward. Given that it's impossible to do so (unless you have a time machine), they risk delaying their decisions indefinitely or never moving forward at all.

This is particularly troublesome for entrepreneurial ventures. When you're building something new, you never have certainty with respect to which choice is the "right" one. Instead, you must study your options, select a path, and forge ahead, willing to live with the consequences and open to changing course if necessary. If you are drowning in data—data that could theoretically give you the answer you're seeking—it's tempting to continue crunching the numbers indefinitely rather than moving forward. The problem is that when you're doing something new, no matter how much data you have at your disposal, you cannot predict the future. If you're an entrepreneur with limited time and resources, falling into the trap of analysis paralysis could prove to be your worst—and your last—mistake.

Optimizing Instead of Innovating

No one *optimizes* themselves into greatness. You can optimize yourself into efficiency, cost-cutting, or restructuring, all of which may be required at various times in the life of a business. But preserving option value and endlessly fine-tuning your analyses before making decisions does not prime you to change the world or blaze a trail. It primes you to preserve the status quo, albeit with slight improvements over time. Leaders must enunciate a vision so that their followers and their teams are able to join them, contribute to the mission, and partake in the benefits of their combined efforts.

In a much buzzed about *New York Times* article, the CEO of a prominent American company implored his employees to take charge of their own destinies—including taking hours of online courses, often on nights and weekends—if they were to develop new skills and remain relevant in the workplace.[9] If you don't keep up, he warned them, your future, much like the fate of the company, is up in the air.

Those weren't the words of Mark Zuckerberg, Ginni Rometty, or Elon Musk, but rather Randall Stephenson, the CEO of AT&T, the seemingly staid Fortune 500 company with a workforce of nearly 300,000 employees. So much for coasting in cushy corporate offices. When one of America's largest companies expects its workers to spend their free time taking online courses to invest in their skills—or else— it's clear that a seismic shift is taking hold. It's understandable why Stephenson is trying to rally his troops to transform AT&T: the telecom pioneer's battle to stay relevant and to compete with tech giants like Amazon and Google will be fought with human capital.

Smart companies get it—either you innovate or you risk being swallowed up or becoming a dinosaur. Despite large corporations' best efforts to spur their employees to act like entrepreneurs, they're failing: 52 percent of firms listed in the Fortune 500 in 2000 have gone bankrupt, been acquired, or ceased operations as a litany of industries have been unmade, reshuffled, and remade by advances in technology.[10] Within the next ten years, the pace of change will only accelerate, with another 40 percent of the current Fortune 500 expected to disappear.[11]

People with FOBO, and by extension the organizations they lead or in which they work, place option value before all else. This means that they are inherently incapable of building *new* things. You cannot innovate when you see the world as a fixed pie and your singular, perhaps compulsive goal is to optimize each decision in order to ensure the biggest and best slice for yourself. To build new things, disrupt industries, and challenge the status quo, companies and their leaders must create incentives to take risks, try new things, and perhaps even fail. This is impossible when a company's culture is drowning in analysis paralysis, hedging, and over-optimization, all of which produce stasis and promote business as usual. FOBO is the antithesis of entrepreneurial thinking.

It's because of FOBO that start-ups beat the odds and surpass large companies. It's why Netflix killed Blockbuster and Amazon is displacing many of America's traditional retailers. While incumbents conduct endless studies, organize countless meetings with Bob in Finance, and generate myriad potential growth or restructuring plans, start-ups come from behind and eat their lunch. When these upstart organizations act, they move quickly and with conviction. They use data to take calculated risks rather than to justify another round of meetings, consultants, and static thinking. Since start-ups work on short timelines and operate with limited resources, they have neither the time nor the money to operate any other way. They must act decisively or it's game over.

Trading Leadership for Inertia

Whether in government, military, or business settings, leaders must assess the challenges that lie before them, determine what they know and what they don't know, and then chart a course forward. They must be decisive, even in the face of uncertainty, risk, and the possibility that they will miss out on an option or forego an opportunity. That is the mark of a leader. In the absence of these qualities, progress can grind to a halt.

FOBO, on its own, can greatly hamper decision-making, but when you combine it with FOMO, it can lead to a Fear of Doing Anything, or **FODA**, and the results can be catastrophic. This phenomenon occurs when your desire to try to do everything (FOMO) crashes into your need to keep all of your options open (FOBO). When you have FODA, you are pulled in two directions at once. Part of you is keen to run in this or that direction in pursuit of something that you perceive to be better and more rewarding than what you have at the moment. At the same time, you are unable to commit to any of those potential options. You aren't sure where to run, and you loathe the notion of settling for just one alternative. As a result, you run around in circles getting nowhere and exhausting yourself in the process. This is a failure of leadership, focus, and commitment, and it condemns you to decision purgatory.

Interestingly, from the moment I started using FODA as part of my vocabulary, I learned that it naturally translates across a few different cultures. If you yell out FODA in Brazil, you'd better be careful of the context. It's the local equivalent of the F Word, a coincidence that feels totally apt. I also recently learned that its translation in the Middle East is even more relevant. When you say the word FODA, most people will think you've actually said "fauda," or the Arabic word فوضى that translates to mean "chaos." If there's one thing that FODA provokes in its sufferers and the people in their orbits, it's most certainly chaos.

Over the last several years, the combined effects of FOMO and FOBO have played out on the world stage through the international incident that is Brexit. Following a referendum in which a slim majority of the British public expressed its desire to exit the European Union (EU), the country's prime minister and parliament have been locked in a painful and often surreal battle to convert the public's will into action. Given the complexities of the issues at hand, the uncertainty of their long-term effects, and the political realities at play, parliamentarians, like the public at large, have been fraught with the FOs.

When British voters went to the polls to support Brexit, part of their calculation was based on FOMO. They were compelled by the perception, fueled by information asymmetry, that breaking free from the EU would offer clear-cut economic and political benefits. By exploiting the gap between perception and reality with a campaign built on misinformation and emotion, the Leave movement mobilized a herd of supporters and won at the polls. The date for the UK's exit was set for March 2019, giving the UK two years to negotiate its departure. Unfortunately, the political realities of separating from Europe have been starkly different than what was sold to the public. Yet even though perception truly was deception, lawmakers must still find a way to turn those FOMO-fueled promises into policy. While many plans and pieces of legislation have been floated, all of them entail trade-offs. That's not a new concept in politics, but in the face of these hard yet necessary choices, British leaders opted for FOBO over action.

In the face of the impending March 2019 deadline to either agree to an exit package or crash out of the EU without a deal, the elected representatives of the people voted against every potential course of action that crossed the floor of their chamber. Instead, they chose to wait for something, anything, that would be better than their existing set of options. As FOMO collided with FOBO and the March deadline blew by, the only affirmative step they took was to request multiple extensions of the deadline, as if by delaying the inevitable, things would magically change. Finally, after three general elections, three deadline extensions, and two prime ministers, parliament passed a Brexit bill in early 2020.

Ironically, as the clock ticked on, the parliament of the UK moved away from finding an optimal solution to the challenge of implementing

Brexit. With no leverage and no time, the focus shifted to damage control. The inability of one of the world's greatest deliberative bodies to make a decision regarding one of the most important issues that has ever come before it has humbled the nation. It's not surprising that more than 80 percent of the British public believes that the country has handled Brexit badly.[12] Time will tell how this unfortunate quagmire ends, but the trauma it has inflicted on the British political system is clear.

As the saga of Brexit shows, no one will ever praise a leader for his or her indecisiveness, especially when there are global implications. Leaders with FOBO are selfish, rather than selfless, in nature. They focus on self-preservation, risk mitigation, meeting their own needs first before worrying about others, and maximizing short-term objectives. While it's quite possible to succeed for a time when you operate with such a set of directives, the long-term prospects are far more dubious. FOMO causes you to make decisions based on emotions while avoiding the cold, hard facts and the realities of the situations. FOBO creates a culture of risk aversion and stagnation, and ultimately leads to a leadership vacuum. When a selfish leader departs, whether of his own choice or not, he leaves behind a rudderless ship.

Why would anyone, especially someone who is capable and ambitious, follow a leader with FOBO? Prime Minister Theresa May found that out the hard way. In the wake of the second deadline extension and a loss of confidence in her leadership, she was forced to resign. Based on the intractable situation in which the UK finds itself, she may not be the last political leader to lose their job because of FOBO.

DECISIVE: CHOOSING WHAT YOU ACTUALLY WANT AND MISSING OUT ON THE REST

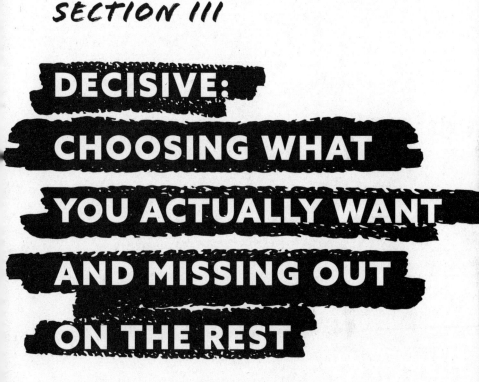

"For what is freedom? That one has the will to assume responsibility for oneself."

—FRIEDRICH NIETZSCHE

CHAPTER 8

Freedom from Fear

"How much I missed, simply because
I was afraid of missing it."
—**PAULO COELHO**

Since 1880, nearly every American president has made use of the *Resolute* desk, either in the Oval Office or in his private study. The story behind how it got to the White House is a fascinating little footnote in history. In 1854, the HMS *Resolute,* part of the British Royal Navy, was abandoned after becoming trapped in the frozen waters of the Canadian Arctic. The ship was assumed lost until sixteen months later when an American whaling vessel overtook an abandoned warship that was listing to one side in the ice floes. It was the *Resolute!* She had drifted over 1,000 miles east, somehow making it relatively unscathed through Baffin Bay toward Greenland.[1] Once rescued, Congress purchased the ship from its scavengers, funded all necessary repairs, and returned her to the Queen. When the *Resolute* was later decommissioned, several desks were produced from her timbers, and Queen Victoria gave one of them to President Rutherford B. Hayes as an expression of gratitude.[2]

For such an illustrious representation of American power, nothing about the origin story of the *Resolute* desk telegraphs the qualities you would actually want in a president. It's quite the opposite. The ship was frozen in place, carried along by currents, and adrift for over a year until it was rescued by a much smaller ship. It sounds like a leader's worst nightmare. That incongruity is precisely why the *Resolute* desk is such an apt metaphor for the tests faced by all leaders. The men (and someday women) who sit at the *Resolute* desk are not uniformly decisive or judicious. They are human, just like you and me, and they make mistakes too. In order to succeed, they must always remain vigilant, resisting the urge to follow the crowd or to delay taking action. The must also find the humility to ask for help. In essence, they must work very hard to be decisive, especially when they know that their decisions will affect millions, if not billions, of people. No desk, not even the one sitting in the Oval Office, makes that task any easier. I will note, however, that Richard Nixon opted not to use the desk. Perhaps that's where his problems began.

Learning to Be Decisive

In this section of the book, we will target the drivers of FOMO and FOBO and explore a series of strategies that will help you to first manage and then eventually neutralize them. The battle you will wage will be comprehensive and will span both the professional and the personal. Given the growing integration between these once very separate realms, you must take a comprehensive approach if you want to position yourself for success. As you do so, you'll soon find that there's no elusive secret to overcoming your FOs. Instead, the key to getting past them is rooted in spotting them, calling them out, and then combatting them in ways big and small. The good news is that this can be done. The strategies you will learn are highly pragmatic, and you can begin implementing them today. No matter how much you struggle with FOMO, FOBO, or both, with sustained commitment, you will soon find that you too can sit at the *Resolute* desk.

Now that your intentions are clear, it's time to convert them into solutions. In order to conquer your FOs and even leverage them for good, you must attack them at the source: you must change the way you make decisions. After all, FOMO is the decision to worry that you're missing out on something. It's the decision to do something or not do something. The decision to be a wildebeest or *not* be a wildebeest. Similarly, FOBO is the struggle to overcome a fear of decision-making. Are you able to accept an outcome that does not maximize all of your criteria? Can you act with conviction when hedging your bets can feel a lot more comfortable? Finally, are you prepared to examine how your behavior impacts you, as well as the people around you?

If all of that sounds a bit daunting, fear not. Indecision has long been catastrophic to careers, companies, and nations. That fact is not in dispute. But although it poses persistent risks and challenges, it's not insurmountable. You can learn how to escape the trap of FOMO and the quagmire of FOBO. To achieve this objective you must be *decisive*. What does success look like? It looks like freedom. When you find the power to choose what you actually want and the courage to miss out on the rest, you are finally liberated from indecision and the compulsion to have it all. Even though you'll be eliminating options, missing out on potential experiences and opportunities, and generally limiting the scope of the things you could potentially do in your life, your overall outlook will improve. You will be more relaxed, in the flow, and free to move forward into the future without regret. Most importantly, when you learn to be decisive, you will be *free from fear*.

That's the thing about FOMO and FOBO that often gets over-looked. They are all about *fear*. When you use their acronyms, as most people do, the word fear doesn't make an appearance, but it's there the whole time, hiding in plain sight, whether you realize it or not. Since these behaviors are rooted in fear, they are also entirely emotional. When you remember that fear and emotion are the drivers of everything you're feeling, things change. No one wants to live a life that is dominated by anxiety and apprehension. That's why it's so important to stand up and declare war.

No war is fought alone. You'll need an army in order to prevail in the heat of the battle. In my crusade against the FOs, I've built my own army of experts to gain new insights that have been critical to clarifying and diversifying my own perspective. In doing so, I've interviewed a wide range of fascinating people on my podcast *FOMO Sapiens* and for this book, whose expertise spans both theory and real-world applications. This includes a neuroscientist who is also a Buddhist meditation teacher, a psychotherapist with an MBA, a bunch of entrepreneurs, a Catholic priest, some venture capitalists, an expert on digital well-being, a research psychologist, my mom, a social media expert, a relationship expert, a behavioral designer, and even a twelve-year-old kid! All of these people have joined me, and now you, on the crusade to replace FOMO and FOBO with freedom from fear.

When Conviction Meets Focus

Now that you know that decisiveness is the destination, it begs an obvious question: What does it take to get there? Learning to act decisively is a multi-stage process. First, you must train yourself to spot and diagnose the FOs and then understand how they manipulate you and undermine your decisions. The good news is that you've already done that work in the previous two sections of this book. Now you will concentrate on (i) choosing what you actually want and then (ii) missing out on the rest. These are the two basic actions you will take to conquer both FOMO and FOBO, and you must tackle each one with a specific set of strategies that you will learn and then practice starting now:

1. *Choosing What You Actually Want* involves knowing what's important to you, prioritizing your objectives, and then operating in a way that allows you to achieve them. When you are able to commit fully to what you *should* be doing rather than fixating on what you *could* be doing, you live life with *conviction*. Conviction is the antidote to both FOMO, where you try to choose everything, and FOBO, where it's so tempting to choose nothing. Chapters 9, 10, and 11 will focus on this objective.

2. *Missing Out on the Rest* means that you will remain on guard for the countless triggers, distractions, and behaviors that will undermine you and sap you of conviction. No matter how hard you work, that's an inevitable fact of modern life and of being human. As a result, you must constantly work to *focus* on what truly matters and then let go of everything else. Chapter 12 will show you how to work toward this goal.

Acting decisively in the context of FOMO and FOBO requires a particular mindset that is distinct from other types of decision-making. When you're dealing with the FOs, you are selecting from a set of favorable options. This isn't like playing the "Would You Rather" game in which you face some gruesome hypothetical like "Would you rather be boiled alive or be eaten by a boa constrictor?" You aren't seeking out the least horrible option, but instead trying to choose just one from among many perfectly acceptable outcomes. It's only when you don't decide on anything and options begin to slip away that things get ugly. That's why you cannot procrastinate. You must choose with conviction from among the many viable candidates at your disposal and then dedicate yourself to sticking with that decision.

Over the next few chapters, as you learn to act with conviction and trade distraction for focus, you will also have to confront your demons. Even once you've resolved to live decisively, the very same forces that hindered you in the first place will still be there, attacking from all sides. It's possible that years of FOMO and FOBO have made you complacent. When indecision becomes habitual, even oddly comfortable, change can feel jarring. If you're easily drawn into the herd, struggle with analysis paralysis, or feel beholden to the status quo, it's natural to resist change. That's why the strategies you will employ are all highly pragmatic in nature. *Practicality is the mortal enemy of fear.* When trying something new is rooted in common sense, it's much easier to embrace it, implement it, and make tangible progress. As you do so, you will start to realize the benefits almost immediately, which will motivate you to continue your efforts.

Becoming decisive is not only about eliminating destructive behavior, it's also about gaining productivity. By operating with conviction and focus, you're also unlocking a lot of upside for yourself. No matter how you cut it, the FOs are a tremendous waste of time and energy. When you no longer must contend with them, you will move through life with far greater speed and efficiency than you might have thought possible. Like an elite athlete or great artist, you'll move up from the ranks of the amateurs and raise your game because all of your efforts, time, and energy will yield so much more.

My sister-in-law, Davalois Fearon, is a dancer and choreographer in New York City. If you ever see Dava in performance, you'll be struck by the efficiency with which she executes her choreography. No movement is wasted, even as she propels her body with a balanced combination of grace and athleticism. This is a virtuous cycle that unites an economy of motion and a unity of purpose. It is the nexus of alignment and flawless execution, perfected through years of practice and hard work. Apply this same precision to how you operate in the world. When you're decisive, each endeavor will contribute to your overall strategy. The more tightly you can align your decisions with your overall objectives, the more you can achieve with each and every action. Greater alignment also increases the chance that you will find success and fulfillment without getting hurt. Through practice and dedication, you will create a virtuous cycle that produces better outcomes and makes you a stronger contributor to your family, your job, and your community. Most importantly, you will enjoy the ride, knowing that you are driving the car rather than riding along as a passenger.

At this point, you might be asking yourself how you can practice each of these strategies in order to master them. I've got very good news for you on that front. Each day, you have hundreds, if not thousands, of opportunities to make decisions of varying levels of consequence. While most of these choices are made subconsciously or don't require much thought, some will trigger bouts of indecision. You can now welcome each of these moments as an invitation to engage in hand-to-hand combat with both FOMO and FOBO and to learn from the experience. You can then hone your skills in a way that causes minimal friction and should not upend your life. As you do so, you can improve, little by little, until you find yourself making decisions far differently than you did before. You will also gradually prepare yourself for the bigger moments, when acting decisively could have meaningful implications. In this way, making decisions is like flexing a muscle. The more that you do it, the stronger you become. If you stick with it, you will someday surprise yourself by lifting far more than you ever thought you could.

It's time to get started. As with any addictive behavior—and both FOMO and FOBO are highly addictive—the first step in recovery is to admit that you have a problem. That means learning to spot your FOs and then owning them. In addition to the diagnostic tests that you took earlier in the book, you will also rely on common sense. If you feel like you are making twenty life-altering decisions a day, that tells you something. Unless you're leading a country or treating gravely ill patients, then life shouldn't be so complicated. You're wasting time, energy, and headspace on things that do not really matter.

On the other hand, if you can sail through the calmer waters of life with relative ease, you will be far more likely to weather the storm. You can say a lot of things about the HMS *Resolute*, but you can't say she wasn't resilient. That is the exceptional quality that set her apart, captured the attention of world leaders, and continues to underscore her legend more than 150 years later. As you'll see in the next chapter, the best way to begin the task of overcoming your FOs is to first tackle the small decisions in life. Once you have done that, you will have the mental strength and resilience you need to strive for conviction when it comes to matters of consequence.

CHAPTER 9

Don't Sweat the Small Stuff

"Life tends to be an accumulation of a lot of
mundane decisions, which often gets ignored."
—DAVID BYRNE

Great leaders are known for their decisiveness. Consider people who
changed the course of history, like Abraham Lincoln, Rosa Parks, and
Mahatma Gandhi. Each one of these legends faced one or more critical
decisions that they made in the face of personal risk or professional peril.
If they had chased after a long list of priorities, vacillated, or failed to
commit, every one of them would have been relegated to the dustbin of
history. Instead, by acting decisively, each unleashed a wave of change
that reshaped the world around them.

While these leaders are judged on the momentous decisions they
made in their lives, they also made an incalculable number of smaller
decisions that never receive any attention, but probably should. If you
cannot deal with the mundane issues, if you sweat the small stuff, you
will have no bandwidth for the matters that really move the needle.

That's not to say that you shouldn't care about the details. Steve Jobs was notoriously meticulous when it came to running Apple, but part of his strength was in knowing which details mattered to him and which did not. For example, the aesthetics of product design were vital to him, while the aesthetics of his own wardrobe were not. He famously wore a black turtleneck, blue jeans, and New Balance sneakers every day so that he could free up time to focus on more important issues. For some people, choosing something to wear every day is a form of self-expression, but for Jobs it was immaterial.

When you have FOMO or FOBO, you sweat the big stuff, the medium stuff, and the small stuff. All the time. Sweating the big stuff is understandable, but when you bring that level of intensity to all of your decisions, you're making your life way more complicated than it should or needs to be. Yet even if you intrinsically understand that a decision most definitely belongs in the province of the trivial, that's cold comfort when you're living in a choice-rich environment that taps into the technological, biological, social, and cultural triggers that drive your FOs. It can be maddening to keep things simple. If you want to buy a pair of shoelaces on Amazon, you'll have to choose from over 2,000 options! That's just one of the daily struggles you must overcome when you live in a world that offers more options than anyone—even the most resolute of shoelace shoppers—can bear.

Setting Priorities: What Are the Stakes?

In order to tackle FOMO and FOBO, you will need to determine *what you actually want* so that you can resist distractions. Although this question can seem deceptively simple on the surface, it's shocking how rarely most people stop to think about what they really want out of life.

That applies to the big things, but it's also a surprisingly common issue when it comes to the innocuous decisions that you make on a daily basis.

That's why the first step to becoming decisive is to think small. I'm a big believer in quick wins, and the surest way to score a bunch of quick wins is to focus your efforts on the small decisions that waste time and provoke unneeded stress and distraction. By doing so, you will simplify your life considerably. If you can make short work of these routine choices, you will gain confidence and build the muscle memory needed to operate with greater conviction when the stakes are higher. This begs a natural question: How do you separate the small or trivial issues from those that will require greater time and effort? It's a matter of prioritization.

Have you ever spent your workday responding to dozens of routine emails only to realize that the crucial items on your to-do list remain untouched? Even though you should be attending to more important matters, it's tempting to occupy yourself with digital housekeeping, which feels productive. Cleaning out your inbox can be very sneaky in that sense. It looks and feels a lot like work, but it's actually a reasonably well-disguised form of procrastination. Whether it comes to your inbox or your marriage, when you divert your attention toward non-consequential issues, you have no time, energy, or patience to sort through bigger and more important matters. That's why it is so important to move quickly beyond the frivolous with as little drama as possible.

Just ask Monsignor Frederick Dolan, who frequently helps people through life's most consequential events. Msgr. Dolan is a bit of an unconventional pastor. He pursued an MBA, and after working as a stockbroker with Merrill Lynch, entered the Catholic priesthood. He is now the Canadian vicar of Opus Dei. Given his line of work, Father Fred has learned through experience that when it comes to actual life-and-death moments, nobody feels the FOs. All of the anxiety and indecision are replaced by clarity. Having seen this countless times, he advises his parishioners not to wait until the next crisis comes along to prioritize what matters. Dolan points to the words of Pope Francis to underscore his message: "Say no to an ephemeral, superficial, and throwaway culture, a culture that assumes that you are incapable of taking on responsibility and facing the great challenges of life!"[1]

The key to prioritization lies in knowing how to think about each point of indecision you face within the context of your overall life. To do so, each time you feel yourself getting stuck, you're going to prioritize based on the stakes of the decision at hand. This will require you to first separate the important from the mundane. You will do this by determining where a particular issue falls within one of three categories: High-Stakes, Low-Stakes, and No-Stakes. Once you know the stakes, you will be able to tailor your strategy to overcome indecision accordingly.

WHAT ARE THE STAKES?

HIGH-STAKES DECISIONS are fundamental strategic determinations that will have important and potentially definitive medium- to long-term impact. They are the choices that you must absolutely get right if you want to thrive. It's unclear, however, which is the best course of action, so they require a structured, deliberative process.

LOW-STAKES DECISIONS are those that will frequently recur in life and business. They relate to things that must happen on a daily basis, and while they are somewhat mundane, they are necessary to make sure that the trains arrive on time, the goods show up on the shelves, and the plants get watered. When it comes to such matters, you can't do just anything. There is a correct answer, in fact, there are probably many, so the challenge lies in choosing just one and sticking with it.

WHAT ARE THE STAKES?

NO-STAKES DECISIONS have zero potential to shake the universe. This includes questions like: "What color shirt should I wear?" or "Should I go for a run today?" These are the minor details of your life, and there are no incorrect answers. These are choices on which you could spend time, but you shouldn't.

At this point, you may be wondering how it's possible to sort all of your decisions into just three categories. You might also be asking yourself why there aren't a bunch of other categories like Medium-Stakes Decisions, Somewhat-High-Stakes Decisions, or Semi-Low-Stakes Decisions. That is exactly the point of the exercise. If you had to sort your decisions into 25 categories, you'd never get anywhere. Your goal is to remove complexity from your decision-making process, not make it more complicated.

You're also not going to tamper with what's already working just fine. Whether you realize it or not, you're already making thousands of decisions successfully every day. Otherwise, you'd struggle to even get out of bed in the morning. When making up your mind is straight-forward, the process can feel manageable, even routine. You probably weren't even aware that you did, in fact, make a decision, since your intuition took over and did its job. When you get stuck, however, every-thing starts to feel important, regardless of the actual gravity of the matter at hand. The stakes feel high, and your intuition is hijacked by the mounting pressure to pick the right option and achieve the perfect outcome. After all, this decision is what's causing you stress and denying you the satisfaction that comes with closure. It's at that point that you inject unnecessary complexity into your decision-making process.

This has got to stop. Your goal is to simplify what's going on in your head, rather than to complicate it. By stepping back and setting priorities, albeit in a broad sense, you begin to remove the emotion from the equation. You'll also soon realize that most decisions are relatively inconsequential and don't merit the stress they provoke. By actively separating Low-Stakes and No-Stakes Decisions from High-Stakes Decisions, you can reclaim the luxury real estate that you have ceded to these very demanding tenants in your cerebral cortex.

Of course, it's important to recognize that what could be a Low-Stakes Decision to one person might matter a lot more to someone else. If you're a presidential candidate picking clothing for the last debate before election day, you'll want to think long and hard about what color shirt you're going to wear. If you're preparing for a marathon, then making time for a run might be critical to keeping your training schedule on track. But those are the exceptions, not the rule. For most people, such matters are of little significance.

As you sort your decisions based on their stakes, you may find that you have doubts from time to time. The definitions for each category are not meant to be exhaustive—they cannot be given the diversity of activities that fill up your schedule. That's why you need to double-check your work. When you've determined that a decision is either Low- or No-Stakes in nature, you will ask three final questions that will serve as a simple gut check so that you can proceed with conviction:

1. Is it ephemeral? Will you have forgotten making this decision in a week (for No-Stakes Decisions) or a month (for Low-Stakes Decisions)?

2. Does the decision have insignificant consequences in terms of money, time, or its impact on yourself and others?

3.   Can you abide by your choice, no matter what the outcome?

Assuming that you can answer each of these questions affirmatively, your deliberation clearly falls into the province of either a Low-Stakes Decision or a No-Stakes Decision. For both Low-Stakes and No-Stakes Decisions, you will learn to address FOMO and FOBO together in the remainder of this chapter. On the other hand, if your answer to any of these questions is no, then you're dealing with a High-Stakes Decision. Given the complexity inherent in matters of consequence, you will need to tackle FOMO and FOBO separately in those cases. You'll learn how in chapters 10 and 11.

Focusing on What Matters, Forgetting What Doesn't

Have you ever asked yourself why you have trouble making insignificant decisions? Maybe you've wondered what might be the root cause of the challenge? While it would be intellectually interesting to know what's going on behind the scenes, for the purposes of this chapter it's irrelevant. Who cares why you cannot decide between the chicken or the fish? Just decide already. When it comes to No-Stakes or Low-Stakes Decisions, it doesn't really matter.

In order to change the way you do things and break old habits, you are going to make a determination that might seem, at first glance, to be counterintuitive: you *are not* going to embark on a deep dive to figure out what's causing your indecision in the first place. To do so would require a considerable investment of time and energy that plays to your worst impulses. If you're habitually indecisive, conducting a forensic audit of your psyche would cause you to procrastinate further. That's not to dismiss the value of understanding your motivations. It's reasonable to assume that if you knew what caused your indecision, you would be better equipped to address it. That's why you're going to engage in a process to do exactly that, but you're going to hold off until it's time to focus on making High-Stakes Decisions in the next two chapters. Those matters are consequential, which justifies the time and effort required to think more deeply about the underlying forces that are driving your behavior.

For Low-Stakes and No-Stakes Decisions, instead of falling into the trap of analysis paralysis when it comes to your own analysis paralysis, you're going to make things very simple for yourself. You're going to focus on action, and you're going to deal with both of the FOs in exactly the same way. Remember, you're trying to reclaim precious mental real estate, not refill it with more noisy and disrespectful tenants. Your primary goal, starting now, is to stop wasting time and instead clear your plate so that you can move on to more important matters. The sooner you move, the better.

Outsourcing as a Way to Beat Your FOs

When you're lying on your death bed, there is zero chance that you're going to look back and wish you had stayed at the Westin instead of the Marriott back in May 2014. But at the time you were making that booking, you might have agonized over it. That's the nasty thing about FOMO and FOBO. They feel so important in the heat of the moment that it's difficult to think dispassionately. This dynamic shows why it's so critical to find a method to strip out the emotion and doubt before they hijack your intuition and bog you down.

The most effective way to do that is to remove yourself from the process. After all, you are the person who is injecting these elements into your deliberations in the first place. The minute you're gone from the picture so is the drama. Given the limited impact of Low-Stakes and No-Stakes Decisions, there is no reason to be risk averse or to try to exert control. You've already determined that they are ephemeral and of limited consequence and that you can abide by any eventual outcome. The relief of *just deciding already* outweighs any potential benefit that would result if you invested time trying to select the optimal outcome. Plus, you're stuck, so who knows how long that would take! As a result, you're better off stepping back and letting someone (or even the universe, as you will see shortly) do the work for you. That's why you're going to outsource the decision.

Outsourcing is a practice in which companies or individuals employ outside suppliers to perform services that they have traditionally handled themselves. Whether you're a busy family or a multinational corporation, it represents a strategic way to recruit help and engage new resources in order to solve your problems. When you outsource, you make a basic calculation about how you're focusing your time and attention: you determine that while you *could* do something yourself, you will be able to lower costs and increase efficiency if you engage someone else to do it. That's why most large companies outsource a meaningful portion of their call center operations. They have learned that when they perform these functions themselves, it's more expensive and less efficient, so they engage a third party instead.

Of course, it is also entirely possible that if these companies invested time and capital into their own call centers, they could potentially keep them in-house. With the right combination of human and financial capital, they may perform as well or even better as a result. But they recognize that the distraction of doing so isn't worth the effort. It's not the highest and best use of their time. Their return on investment will be higher if they opt for efficiency and a perfectly good outcome instead of a chance at perfection. They will then redirect their resources into initiatives that have the potential to generate higher returns.

The same goes for you. Although it's possible that investing your own precious time and resources into the minor decisions in life could lead to slightly better decisions, the return on investment is just not there. A small improvement on a Low-Stakes or No-Stakes Decision doesn't move the needle enough. That's why you too will outsource. You will engage external resources to break the logjam, increase efficiency, and lower the cost of making decisions.

No-Stakes Decisions: Ask the Watch

When it comes to matters that are completely inconsequential, any outcome is completely acceptable, since there is no incorrect answer. The only bad choice you can make is to waste more than a minute making up your mind. You need to choose one thing and go with it. While you can certainly ask someone else for guidance, you risk wasting even more time seeking feedback. Plus, if you bother the people around you for advice on such minor issues, you will undermine your credibility as a leader. If you have a reputation as someone who cannot deal with the small stuff, then how can anyone trust you when the stakes are higher? There is a solution to this dilemma, but you will need to have an open mind. You'll be putting your fate in the hands of the universe or, more precisely, the hands of your watch.

When I was a sophomore in college, my friend Francesca introduced me to a concept that has served me ever since the day I first learned about it. One day in our dorm, I was agonizing over something stupid. It was so minor that I have zero recollection as to what could have been so vexing to my sophomoric (literally) existence. It was probably something like:

"Should I study now and have lunch later, or should I have lunch now and study later." Yes, as you can see, back in college I was a complex and tortured soul.

After watching me deliberate for twenty minutes or so, Francesca gave me a lifeline. She told me to "ask the watch." Here's how it works. First, you whittle down your decision until you arrive at a simple yes/ no or either/or choice. This is known as a closed-ended question. For example, you ask, "Should the font size be 11 or 12?" or "Should I do the client dinner at this restaurant or that one?" You're still allowing yourself to entertain a few potential outcomes, but you're limiting the realm of possibilities to a manageable few, any of which is acceptable. Next, you assign each of these outcomes, yes/no or either/or, to one half of the face of your watch. For example, "yes" corresponds to the right half of the watch face, where the second-hand falls between 1 and 30, while "no" corresponds to the other half. That established, you look down, read the time, and do whatever the watch says you should do. If you don't have a watch, you can use a cellphone and make your decision based on whether the minute is even or odd when you check the time. You can also split the watch face into three, four, or more options if needed. That's what makes the watch preferable to, say, flipping a coin. You give yourself the flexibility to add a few more options to the mix.

Since I've started asking the watch, I've discovered that making small, insignificant decisions no longer consumes mindshare or calories. I actually find it comforting. In a weird way, it's like the watch, in its infinite wisdom, knew what I wanted the whole time. It's also a quirky routine that makes life a little more interesting. Although I've been careful to restrict my queries to ones that won't be life changing, I've also never gone against the watch's directive. I have no idea what would happen if I contradicted the universe's choice for my in-flight meal. I also don't intend to find out. I have, however, looked down to find that the second hand is right on 30 or 60, which means that the watch is having its own battle with the FOs. In that case, I wait a few minutes and try again. I've never failed to get a clear answer the second time around.

Low-Stakes Decisions: Delegate to Your Squad

Unlike No-Stakes Decisions, when you're dealing with Low-Stakes Decisions there is a correct answer. In fact, there are multiple reasonable courses of action; it's just that when you consider their potential outcomes, the differences between them are relatively small. You have the experience and the knowledge to surface these options, and you can then set parameters and determine what an acceptable outcome should look like. As a result, you already easily dispatch most Low-Stakes Decisions on your own without needing to look for help to do so. At times, however, your FOs will complicate the process. Even if you have come up with a set of perfectly reasonable options, there will be times when you are unable to choose from among them. In these cases, FOMO will cause you to try to do everything while FOBO will keep you from choosing anything, lest the outcome is sub-optimal.

As with No-Stakes Decisions, the Low-Stakes Decisions that you encounter on an ongoing basis offer you the opportunity to outsource your decision-making. By doing so, you can liberate yourself from matters that waste your time, distract your focus, and enable your inner control freak. In this case, however, you will need brainpower on your side, as the outcomes of these choices do have implications that are not entirely inconsequential. Here your approach will be to delegate to someone in your orbit who is equipped to make the decision on your behalf. You can choose to present them with a closed-ended question, but you can also pose an open-ended question, albeit with parameters that set the boundaries and serve as guidelines. Rather than asking "Should we run this analysis or that analysis?" you instead ask, "Can you suggest an analysis that will allow us to determine whether this project makes sense?" The decision-maker will then be empowered to use your parameters to determine which outcome is acceptable and can present a recommendation. Perhaps they will even suggest an approach that you hadn't thought of in the first place.

If you think about it, you are constantly surrounded by individuals you can call on for help. In the context of work, this includes colleagues or administrative staff, while outside of work, this encompasses your partner, family, friends, or other people you trust to be honest with you and who have your best interests at heart. Taken together, these are the people in your squad. While it may seem like Leadership 101, calling upon this valuable resource to help you when it comes to Low-Stakes Decisions may not seem obvious to you if you struggle with the FOs. If you are caught up in the emotional elements of decision-making, you might forget that you can ask for help to push past the point of indecision. Doing so can be essential.

Early in my career, one of my first bosses, a woman named Susan Segal, taught me the value of delegation. I was working as a venture capitalist in Latin America, and our team of ten people managed hundreds of millions of dollars and dozens of investments spread across the region. On a given day, members of the team were working from New York, Buenos Aires, São Paulo, Mexico City, and Miami. With such a small and dispersed organization and with so much to get done, there was little in the way of hand-holding. You were expected to roll up your sleeves, step up, and contribute, irrespective of the title on your business card. A few weeks into my tenure, Susan asked me to get on a plane and figure out how to position one of the companies in our portfolio to raise millions of dollars for a new round of capital. Unbeknownst to me, I was already part of her squad. When she gave me my marching orders, I was terrified. Why would she let a 23-year-old analyst take charge of something so important?

Although I was surprised the first time Susan asked me to step outside of my comfort zone, the experience was hardly unique during the three years that I worked for her. I soon realized that she empowered the people on her team, compelled them to take risks, and held them accountable. Also, what seemed like a huge responsibility to me at the time was actually relatively low-stakes in nature. Susan was an expert at her job and could spot errors or moments of poor judgment. She didn't need to be mired in the weeds to know whether we were making informed decisions or not. We could come to her with ideas, good or bad, and she would work with us and guide us based on her experience. The only thing that was not acceptable was to be wishy-washy or to fail to make a sincere and thoughtful effort to tackle the issues that came across our desks each day. Our culture was one that demanded that we act, and act with conviction. No FOs allowed.

By delegating when it came to Low-Stakes Decisions, Susan gave herself more time and freedom to make the High-Stakes Decisions that fell on her shoulders. She also did herself a big favor by trusting the people on her team—she had hired us after all—to do their jobs. As we gained experience, we could provide her with deeper insights and better counsel with which to manage the business. While this approach was beneficial to Susan, I also came to realize that by empowering me over and over again, she was training me from an early stage in my career to be decisive. She was an unselfish leader, and it paid dividends for all of us.

Outsourcing to your squad offers several benefits. As Susan taught me, doing so frees you up for more important issues. If you are a control freak and you obsess when it comes to Low-Stakes Decisions, you will never be able to succeed in a demanding workplace. Leaders must delegate. Second, it helps you to build a team of decisive, confident individuals who are comfortable exercising their judgment and embracing autonomy. Of course, not all decisions are equally important, so when the stakes are relatively low, you can also empower people who are less experienced to flex their decision-making muscles. Keep in mind that what may seem like a minor issue to you might feel like a big responsibility to someone else, like a junior professional at work or your school-aged child. As you allow others to take charge, they will gain confidence, take manageable risks, and learn from their successes and mistakes. You will be paying it forward by giving them a free education in what it means to be decisive.

Remember, however, that when you delegate, you should always set basic parameters, framed within either an open- or closed-ended question, and then maintain an open line of communication with the person or people you have empowered to take action. After all, your guidance might provide them with critical support or a gentle push if they too struggle to act decisively. Additionally, avoid the temptation to canvass. You only need to ask one person to help you with a Low-Stakes Decision. Anything more will complicate matters. If you do want to engage more than one person, you can ask them to present you with a joint recommendation.

Delegating to your squad doesn't have to remain tethered to the office. You can also bring the same set of strategies into the rest of your life. If you're agonizing over where to go on a date, how to dress for an interview, or where to put your new couch, you're far better off getting out of your head. Accept the fact that you are going to spend way too much time and energy trying to choose one option over another. Also, accept that you're not an expert when it comes to the particular decision that you're making. That's why you need to get into somebody else's head.

Everyone has that friend who has great style, knows every new restaurant in town, or always provides the most sensible advice when it comes to the daily challenges of life. Since these people don't "work" for you, simple delegation won't do the trick. Instead, when you find yourself facing an impasse, you'll call on these people, the subject-matter experts in your squad, who are best equipped for the task at hand. When you engage with them, you're prepared to take their advice and follow it, thus saving yourself from an endless back-and-forth about something that doesn't merit such an investment of effort. As an added benefit, you might find that you end up venturing outside of your comfort zone. By drawing upon the expertise of others and posing open-ended questions, you will learn new things and enjoy the benefits that come from asking for help. Just remember, you too are an expert on a few things as well, so make sure to return the favor when your squad comes calling. Even if you struggle with the FOs when it comes to your own decisions, you'll find that helping others is typically far easier. Since these choices affect somebody else, you can be far more objective and far less emotional than you are when you're dealing with yourself.

While the strategies laid out in this chapter will allow you to drive toward decisions as efficiently as possible, they don't deal with the core issues that foster indecision. It goes without saying that if the stakes are high, you will need a different approach. You clearly shouldn't rely on your watch for the answers. Similarly, you'd be shirking your duties by delegating to someone else. You will need to think deeply, gather data, and then make a decision based on reason, rigor, and experience. You will need to step up and be the protagonist.

As you will see in the next two chapters, when it comes to High-Stakes Decisions, you will take the time to step back and think about the factors that are preventing you from acting decisively. You will also tackle each of the FOs separately, starting with FOMO and then moving on to FOBO. The nature of each of these challenges is different, so to overcome them, you will need to deploy a distinct set of targeted strategies for each one. By tackling the FOs from the bottom up, you will better understand why you get stuck and then build a base of knowledge that will serve you when you wrestle with the same set of issues in the future.

CHAPTER 10

FOMO Is for the Planets, Not the Sun

"The secret to greatness is being indecisive."
—SAID NO ONE EVER

When you have FOMO, you are revolving around someone else's solar system rather than taking your rightful position at the center of your own. This becomes clear when you unpack the emotions that are unleashed when it attacks. You're minding your own business and living your life, when suddenly, BOOM, you're triggered. You hear, read, see, or think of something that starts you obsessing about that thing you're missing out on. Then, without warning, reference anxiety kicks in. As you fixate on whatever is driving your FOMO, you are also subconsciously devaluing everything that you do have. Instead of appreciating all of the good things you've got going, you're laser-focused on some present inadequacy.

FOMO causes you to feel as if your life is not up to snuff based on a bunch of notions that probably don't even correspond to reality. This gap between what you have and what you wish you had is what drives negativity, stress, and unhappiness. The more time you spend building up those feelings, the worse things get since reality will never be able to compete with your imagination. When you allow reference anxiety to run amok, you have weaponized the asymmetry of information behind FOMO and used it to attack yourself. While falling into this trap will rob you of conviction even when it comes to insignificant issues, when you're dealing with High-Stakes Decisions it can inflict great harm.

To face FOMO head-on when it matters most, you must start by addressing this harmful disconnect between perception and reality. This will allow you to rescue your intuition from its captors so that your deliberations are once again fact-based rather than emotional. You can systematically do so by addressing the two types of FOMO that were identified earlier:

1. Aspirational FOMO, which is driven by the *perception*, enabled by an asymmetry of information, that a thing or experience is better than what you have in front of you at the moment; and

2. Herd FOMO, which is fed by a desire for *inclusion* and a compulsion to partake in what you feel you're missing.

In this chapter, you will learn to employ a structured decision-making process that will rob Aspirational FOMO and Herd FOMO of their power so that you can make decisions independently of their influences. As you do so, you will build a set of decision-making skills that will serve you both in this chapter as well as in the next chapter, when you take on FOBO.

Eliminating the Information Asymmetry in Aspirational FOMO

Way back in the Dark Ages, if you came down with an illness, you were in for a harrowing experience. Depending on how you were feeling, your treatment might have included a combination of charms, blood-letting via leeches, mercury pills, and animal dung ointments. Worse, if you suffered from migraines or depression, your doctor would literally drill a hole in your head to expose the outer layer of your brain![1] In the absence of science to suggest a physiologically sound treatment, providers of medical care filled the gap with faith and superstition. Thankfully, research and facts have long supplanted these methods, and no reputable doctor would think of prescribing them today.

That's the beauty of facts. They give you power, prevent you from doing something senseless, and allow you to exercise judgment based on data rather than speculation, emotion, or blind faith. That's not to say that there's no room for trusting in the unknown or letting your heart rule your head. Some things cannot be fact-based. Affairs of the heart will always have a meaningful emotional component. Matters of religion will always be rooted in faith. That goes without saying. But when it comes to dealing with FOMO, you need speculation and conjecture like you need a hole in the head. That's why you must endeavor to operate in the world of cold, hard, observable facts.

The factors that trigger FOMO may vary, but the emotions that they provoke are always the same. You see something you just have to do or have for yourself. Then, you feel all kinds of feelings, things like longing, regret, jealousy, stress, and even failure as Aspirational FOMO kicks in. What you don't feel, however, is absolute certainty about what exactly you're missing. How can you know what you're missing if you haven't even tried it? Unless you're a clairvoyant (another favorite of medical practitioners in the Dark Ages), there is a gaping void between what's going on in your head and what's happening (or will happen) in the real world. Even if you're dealing with an experience or opportunity that's familiar to you—perhaps it's something you've done in the past—how can you be sure that things will be as you imagine this time around? It's at this point that you need to make a decision. Are you going to fill that void with daydreams, speculation, and emotion, or are you going to fill it with facts? The minute you elevate information above speculation, you begin to take control.

As you've seen, venture capitalists have chosen a line of work that requires them to constantly battle their FOs. If your FOMO compels you to invest in everything you see, you'll quickly find yourself in a herd of wildebeests. If your FOBO holds you back from committing, you will be doomed to inaction and a permanent place on the sidelines. To overcome these impulses, great investors adhere to a clear and replicable process that allows them to accumulate the knowledge they'll require to act with conviction.

That's why you're going to start thinking like an investor. If you think about it, you are already investing a lot of time and energy into your FOMO without getting a return. Why not flip the script to make smarter investments with these resources? Of course, you won't be a FOMO-driven wildebeest investor who is playing with someone else's money or is too rich to care if they lose their principal or their principles. You will deliberate with rigor. After all, this is your time, money, and energy, not someone else's. Before you begin, it's important to understand the basic rules of the road that will guide you as you work:

OVERCOMING FOMO WHEN MAKING
HIGH-STAKES DECISIONS

KEEP AN OPEN MIND: Don't fall in love with whatever is giving you FOMO or presume a given outcome.

KNOW WHAT MATTERS: Set criteria to determine if an opportunity meets your objectives.

RELY ON FACTS, NOT EMOTIONS: Compile sufficient data before making a decision.

GATHER DATA FROM MULTIPLE SOURCES: Don't make a decision in a vacuum. Draw on the people around you—and perhaps those beyond your immediate circle—to get information and advice.

Now that you've got some core guidelines in place, it's time to start the processes of stripping away the FOMO from High-Stakes Decisions.

Step 1: Formulate the Question

Your first step is to clearly articulate the option or opportunity that's giving you FOMO. This will be essential to gathering data and establishing your criteria. Take a few moments to clarify your thinking and then formulate the question you're trying to answer as directly and concisely as possible. This could be something like: "Should I interview for the job in California?" or "Should I quit my job to launch an entrepreneurial venture?"

Step 2: Set Criteria to Frame Your Decision

In order to make any decision, you must set parameters that will determine whether a given opportunity meets your standards. This will require you to set some basic criteria. As you do so, endeavor to keep your list of requirements concise and be sure to include these five critical questions:

1. *Can I justify this choice?* Can I list at least five good reasons why I want to have or do this?

2. *Can I afford this?* How much will this cost? What else could I do with my money?

3. *Can I make this choice without sacrificing other, more important, goals?* Do I have time for this? How else could I invest my time and energy?

4. *Can I see a clear return on investment if I choose this option?* What am I going to get out of this? Is it tangible, emotional, or both?

5. *Can I actually make this happen?* Is this opportunity even available to me, or should I be focusing on other opportunities that are also attractive but far more realistic?

Step 3: Gather Data

The key to overcoming Aspirational FOMO is to remove emotion from your deliberations and instead tether your thinking to data and analysis. When an investor tries to figure out whether an opportunity meets her criteria, she conducts an exercise known as due diligence. It's basically like studying for a test. You want to master the topic to such an extent that you could theoretically stand up and teach the class if the professor asked you to. In due diligence, you ask hard questions, gather as much information as possible, and try to chip away at the asymmetry of information that is clouding your judgment. As you undertake this exercise, you will not operate in a vacuum. You will reach out to other people—particularly people who have relevant expertise—in order to expand your perspectives. Just be wary of canvassing more than a few good sources. You don't want risk disguising procrastination as progress.

Step 4: Write It Down

Now that you've got the main areas of inquiry covered, you're going to take another page out of the playbook of the investment community. As investors conduct due diligence, they produce a memo of their findings and then draw some conclusions and a recommendation based on the information. While you could answer the questions listed above in your head, you're going to instead jot down your responses and make, in a sense, your very own due diligence memo. Committing your thoughts to paper provides two distinct advantages. First, by writing something down, you make it tangible, and you're forced to think through your logic. You're invested in the answers, they become concrete the minute they hit the page, and you're less tempted to equivocate. Second, you will keep this list for future reference. If you decide to move forward and invest your time, energy, or money to go after that thing that gave you FOMO, you can later revisit your analysis. By understanding how effectively you conducted your due diligence and your decision-making process, you can improve for next time.

Step 5: Make a Preliminary Judgment

My brother once gave me a valuable piece of advice: the only thing that you control when you're moving through the world is your reaction to what happens around you. By conducting due diligence and then injecting some precision into your thinking, you are taking control. You are eliminating information asymmetry as much as possible in order to make an informed, rather than an emotional, decision. If you cannot come up with five reasons to interview for that job, then don't. If you don't have the money or the time to start that entrepreneurial venture, then you've learned something important. Your heart might still wish you could go after that dream, but your head knows that it's not possible right now and that it's time to move on. Even if you cannot answer all of your questions definitively, you will have far more information than you had before you started. Plus, if you cannot answer these basic questions, that tells you a lot about how much more work you will need to do to close the gap between perception and reality.

You can now begin to draw an initial conclusion based on your work. If the answer is no, then the process ends here. There's no need to proceed if your Aspirational FOMO has now been neutralized as a result of your efforts. On the other hand, if you're still uncertain or you think the answer is yes, then you will proceed to the second part of the process. It's time to wrestle with your Herd FOMO by asking yourself one last essential question.

The Ultimate Gut Check to Escape the Herd

When you're a kid, your parents, your teachers, and pop culture relentlessly remind you to be yourself, find your own way, and never give in to peer pressure. That's also the theme of just about every Disney movie ever made. Whether it's Ariel in *The Little Mermaid,* Belle in *Beauty and the Beast,* or Miguel in *Coco,* the arc of the protagonist's journey requires them to overcome the naysayers, escape the herd, and learn to be themselves. You likely got the same message from your mom, who never failed to remind you of that universal litmus test of being your own person: "If so-and-so jumped off a bridge, would you jump too?" It required a lot of courage, but you took the message to heart. You tried to be yourself, even when it wasn't easy, and you learned that it was OK to be a little different and do your own thing.

It's ironic, then, that FOMO can undo *all* of that hard work. Before you know it, you're right back in the herd, the place you worked so hard to escape. Except now, the stakes are even higher. Unlike your teenage years, when you fell prey to jocks and cheerleaders, this time companies, celebrities, and influencers are out to manipulate you. They want your money, your mindshare, and your likes—and they're willing to play dirty to get them. Do you think of yourself as a follower? I can guarantee you something: they most certainly do. That's the problem with following the crowd. It distracts you from what you *should* be doing and causes you to instead focus on what *everyone else* is doing. It tempts you to make choices that are completely inauthentic, and it impedes you from giving your all to the path that best corresponds to your inner compass.

The absolute worst place you can end up, the destination that is truly tragic, is the place where you feel FOMO for something you don't even actually want. You've taken cues from someone else, whether it's a social media influencer or simply one of the people around you who influences the way you think, and your judgment is now clouded. If you end up getting exactly what you thought you wanted and you feel miserable, that's a pretty horrific outcome. That's why when it comes to disarming FOMO, tackling Aspirational FOMO is not enough. Before you move forward with any High-Stakes Decision, you must also ask yourself one additional question:

Do I actually want to do this, or am I just following the herd?

That's your gut check. It keeps your due diligence honest, keeps you on track, and makes sure that you don't chase after somebody else's or the herd's dreams. It ties you back to your values and the things you care about most. Sometimes it's acceptable to follow the crowd, but if you're going to do so, you should know what you're doing and why.

One tried-and-true method to ensure that you steer clear of the herd is to make sure that you are never part of it in the first place. If the people around you all look, act, and think pretty much the same way as you, you're likely in the danger zone. As a result, even if you're trying very hard to make a decision based on the merits, you run the risk of taking your cues from people who see the world in a very similar way. The result, a pervasive tendency toward groupthink, can end up pulling you back into the herd without you even realizing it. That's why it's critical to seek advice from a diverse set of people when you're making decisions.

Shan-Lyn Ma is the cofounder and CEO of Zola, an online wedding registry that is one of the fastest-growing e-commerce companies in the United States. The company has raised $140 million and was named among the next wave of unicorns by the *New York Times* in 2019. Part of the secret to its success has been Shan's conviction that a diverse senior management team will make smarter, more innovative decisions. As a result, her hiring practices have emphasized diversity—in terms of gender, race, religion, and sexual orientation—since day one. More than half of the senior management team is composed of women, a statistic that is an outlier in the technology industry. She credits the diversity throughout the company as one of its core competitive advantages. By having a DNA that is different than its competitors, Zola has been able to think differently, avoid the herd, and quickly take market share in an industry that is dominated by powerful incumbents.

Now that you have conducted due diligence, weighed your findings against the criteria, and validated the motivations for your reasoning, you are ready to decide. You have undertaken a clear and structured process, and you should have the information you need to act decisively. This is great news, right? While beating FOMO sounds good on paper, making big decisions is tough, even if you've taken all the right steps to do so. If you're still stuck, don't worry; that's a fixable problem. You still have work to do, but closure is within sight.

What If You're Still Stuck?

Let's assume that you've followed all of the steps in this chapter. In order to address Aspirational FOMO, you have conducted thorough due diligence, gathering facts by researching the opportunity and talking to people to fill the holes in your analysis. You have also thought carefully about the range of motivations that are shaping your mindset in order to combat Herd FOMO. Finally, you've written everything down and saved a copy of it in the cloud so that you can keep it for future reference. Nicely done! For most High-Stakes Decisions, you now have the clarity you'll need to make a decision with a high degree of conviction. Let's assume, however, that you're still stuck. What now?

While you are admittedly still paralyzed by indecision, you are in a very different place than you were before you started this process. You have taken the time to think through both your rationale and your motivations, and you have gathered facts to back up your assertions. As a result, you have removed much of the information asymmetry—and a good degree of the risk—from the situation. You will never have perfect information and you cannot predict the future, but you are going in with your eyes wide open, and you can trust your intuition. At this point, your FOMO has given way to inertia. You're stuck for no good reason, and your only escape is to take action. Since you worked hard to find a reason to say no and didn't find a good one, you should feel comfortable saying yes. It's time to go for it. Making any decision requires you to take a calculated risk, and you're in a good position to do so.

When you employ a rigorous process, you're no longer simply giving in to your FOMO. Instead, you listened to your FOMO, learned from it, and then, after a thoughtful process, determined that this time around, FOMO was a force for good. There is always a risk that things won't turn out your way, but that's life, and life entails some measure of risk. The important thing is that your decision was made by you and not by your FOMO. If you are still unsure that you're ready to jump in feet first, you can also consider starting small, testing the waters, and then seeing how you progress before jumping in wholeheartedly. As you will see in chapter 13, you can make FOMO work for you by listening to it and then pursuing some of your interests on a part-time basis.

Now that you have a broad set of tools to manage your FOMO, it's time to turn to FOBO. When you have FOBO, you are so unwilling to take risks that nothing can shake you into action. While some of the strategies you learned in this chapter will be applicable in the next, overcoming FOBO requires a distinct approach that is particularly directed toward *how* you make decisions. As you'll soon learn, while FOMO is deeply rooted in emotions, FOBO is all about process.

CHAPTER 11

Choosing Action over Option Value

"[Every decision] is a risk...threatened by the excluded possibilities, many of which might have been better and truer than the chosen one."
—PAUL TILLICH

If anyone understands FOBO, it's Yael Melamed. After graduating from college, she started her career in strategy consulting before deciding that the next logical step was to pursue a JD/MBA. At that time, Yael wasn't at all sure what she wanted to do with her life, so she decided to spread her bets. She figured that by getting both a law degree and a business degree, she would have lots of options from which to choose. In a future full of uncertainty, option value provided a hedge against any fears of the unexpected. Everything changed when she was diagnosed with skin cancer. In an instant, she realized that she'd had it all wrong. Now that she faced a stark and frightening moment of uncertainty, she lamented that she'd spent way too much time building her résumé and the option value that came with it. Even as she excelled by staying firmly on the choice-rich professional treadmill that was standard among her peers, she never figured out what she truly wanted out of life.

When you face a crisis, you either collapse or you take the setback as an opportunity to make some important decisions. After she received her diagnosis, Yael spent a lot of time thinking about the choices, or perhaps the lack of choices, she had made until that point. Fortunately, her cancer was treatable, and after one surgery she had a clean bill of health. Still, after overcoming such a frightening experience at a young age, she realized that she didn't want to live with fear and regret. She also embraced the notion that life is too short not to be happy each day. As a result, she decided to pursue her calling as a psychotherapist and executive coach. In this new career, she spends her days helping others to find their true selves and then align their lives accordingly.

As a reminder, FOBO is characterized by two distinct yet powerful impulses: (i) *holding out for something better* and (ii) *preserving option value*. In order to withstand these dual pressures when it comes to High-Stakes Decisions, you're going to need to examine how you are currently making the important decisions in your life. You will then reengineer your approach to make it work better. That doesn't mean that you're going to throw all criteria and standards out the window in order to solve your problems. In fact, if you were worried that the solution to FOBO is to settle for just about anything, fear not. It turns out that FOBO is more about your decision-making process than it is about your ultimate objectives. It's still acceptable to want the best, but you have to be careful in how you go about getting it.

To start, it's instructive to revisit what's going on when you feel FOBO. As you'll recall, it originates with the desire to have the best—to maximize—and an aversion to settling for second best. When it comes to these impulses, a recent study by researchers at the University of Waterloo reframed the conversation about FOBO in a rather interesting way.[1] In their findings, the authors asserted that the negative outcomes associated with maximizers are not driven by the end goal of maximization itself. Rather, they are a side effect of the *process* that you use to seek out the alternatives you will consider in your search. Put simply, if you want to avoid feeling FOBO, you have to separate what you *want* from what you *do* to try to get it. Specifically, you must avoid the temptation to keep returning, over and over again, to options that you have already eliminated or passed over. It's this act—revisiting the same set of options—that is so toxic. Even if you don't realize it, each time you reconsider a discarded alternative, you are trading action for option value. This behavior is the psychological equivalent of endlessly flipping through TV channels to see if something better is on, even if you're already fine with what you're watching. If you find channel surfing frustrating, think about how it feels when that's your approach to every big decision you make.

Could the true genesis of FOBO be the desire to preserve option value rather than the instinct to maximize? If you think about it, it makes sense. Lots of effective leaders strive for the best yet never give in to FOBO. Great companies maintain an unshakable commitment to excellence without falling victim to analysis paralysis and stasis. These individuals and organizations are able to shoot for the best and yet still manage to commit to something because they do not get bogged down in the decision-making process. They accept the reality that you must, in fact, decide if you are going to have any shot at success. They also possess the wisdom to know that they must simultaneously let go of other potential options in order to move forward.

If you are to follow their example, then you must accept that you cannot have everything and that you must resolve to jettison all of your options but one. This is not a painless experience. As you eliminate alternatives, you will suffer the small losses that are a natural by-product of eliminating possibilities and shutting doors, some of which might be very tempting. You might even feel a sense of grief as all of those figs from *The Bell Jar* pile up around your feet. But unless you are able to accept these losses and move on, you'll remain stuck, pondering the overwhelming number of branches that are blocking the path forward. That's why overcoming FOBO when it comes to High-Stakes Decisions will employ a process in which you eliminate options and then find the will to let them go. In that way, you will be able to pare your choices down to one, which you will then select with conviction.

How to KonMari Your Mind

If you're going to accept that you cannot have it all, then you must first find a way to dispose of each unexplored option before moving on to your ultimate choice. Even if you're confident that you still have plenty of other good—or even better—options at your disposal, letting go of any of them can still present a major obstacle. Eliminating possibilities can be dispiriting, especially if you're conditioned to think that you can and should have it all. What's the point of living in a choice-rich environment if you cannot take advantage of it? The problem is that you are living in clutter. Just as you wouldn't want to overstuff your closet with tons of clothing that you will never have time to wear, so it is with opportunities. The more clutter you create, the less you'll enjoy any of them.

If you want to eradicate the clutter in your head, you can take a lesson from Marie Kondo, the Japanese tidying guru, who has built a global empire on the power of cleaning up in the home. Her KonMari method of eliminating clutter includes two key concepts. First, in order to simplify your life, you should gather your possessions and then get rid of anything that doesn't "spark joy."[2] Second, before tossing anything out, you should thank it for its service so that you do not feel a sense of guilt when you let it go. It is this second concept that is particularly apt when you're seeking to eliminate options, particularly as you work to set aside the psychological value you ascribe to option value.

While Kondo's methodology may sound a little out there the first time you hear it, she makes an interesting point. As you'll recall, FOBO is an affliction of abundance. If you don't have options, you'll never have to worry about indecision. That's why it's good to recognize that you are very fortunate to have so many opportunities in the first place. You don't have space for all of them at the moment, and they're creating confusion and holding you back, but you're still grateful. If you acknowledge that fundamental reality, it will be easier to relinquish what you don't need without feeling guilt or regret. Just as you can KonMari your closets, you can also KonMari your mind.

If you need some background music to "spark joy" while you do so, you can look to the singer, songwriter, social media influencer, and—stay with me here—modern-day philosopher Ariana Grande for inspiration. If you thought her smash hit "thank u, next" was all about her high-profile breakups with guys like the comedian Pete Davidson, then you missed the true message in the lyrics. It's actually the ultimate anti-FOBO rallying cry. In the song, Grande explains that each time she ended a relationship, she learned something from it, and in doing so, she came to realize that her most important relationship is with herself. For a song that repeats the lyric "I'm so f*ckin' grateful for my ex" six times, that message is *surprisingly* deep. It's also a great strategy to pare down a long list of alternatives to drive toward a decision. In order to eliminate options, you must be prepared to dismiss them one by one and then pick the winner. You cannot look back and second-guess yourself or feel regret. You need to *move on.*

Yael Melamed has her own strategy for getting to "thank u, next" when she's trying to choose from multiple options. Rather than wondering if an option is "good enough," she flips the question around and instead asks, "Is there enough good?" By taking this approach, she no longer measures each decision against some abstract and idealized goal. Instead, she evaluates each alternative on its own merits and proceeds from there. When you focus on the positive attributes of an option rather than the negative, you are more likely to be happy with your eventual decision.

While Marie Kondo, Ariana Grande, and Yael Melamed's strategies all provide some good food for thought, sifting through all of the possibilities in front of you and discarding some as you go isn't always a straightforward endeavor. These calculations can be difficult when there is information asymmetry, and it's hard to gather information to inform your decision. Even when you're dealing with matters that involve data, you must accept the fact that life is not a laboratory. Data isn't always black-and-white, and you can never truly predict what will happen in the future. Plus, when you have FOBO, you're already prone to analysis paralysis, so as you gather information, you're basically picking up kryptonite.

That's why when it comes to High-Stakes Decisions, there are typically no easy answers and there is no magic bullet. Instead, you've got to strap on your seat belt and face them head-on. To do so, you're going to need to accept that this could take hours or days of work rather than minutes. Given the nature of FOBO, you must also think in terms of process rather than outcome alone. As you saw in the last chapter, developing a clear strategy will introduce rigor into your thinking while making you more effective and efficient. It is a worthwhile investment of energy that will pay dividends: you will be able to follow the same set of steps time after time and, as with any learned skill, you will refine and improve your approach as you go along.

The Process of Being Decisive

Now that you know how to shift your mindset when it comes to option value, you're ready to apply this outlook to making High-Stakes Decisions. Part of overcoming FOBO comes with practice. As you gain life experience and professional acumen, problems that would have been daunting in the past suddenly seem reasonably solvable. It's like merging into the traffic on a busy highway. When you're just starting out, it can feel like you're driving a scooter while everyone else is speeding along in a state-of-the-art electric vehicle. The chances of making a wrong move and going splat are perilously high. Then, as you gain experience, two things happen. First, you are more prepared to make smart decisions. You trade up your scooter for something better until one day, you might even command that long-awaited electric Audi if they ever get their act together. Second, you start to see everything with far less fear. What looked like a race car when you were twenty can seem like a Matchbox ten years later. With perspective, the gap between the many challenges in your life and your capacity to solve them yourself shrinks to the point where it's no longer an obstacle. Your experience makes all the difference.

How do you move up the experience curve when it comes to making High-Stakes Decisions? In the last chapter, you learned how to conduct due diligence in order to determine whether to take advantage of a given opportunity. You will once again use this approach to move past indecision. This time, however, you will come at your analysis from a different perspective. Unlike with FOMO, you're not trying to determine whether one option or opportunity meets your criteria. On the contrary, when you have FOBO, the challenge is that you already have more good options than you can handle. If you're ever going to be able to choose just one of them, you must engage in a process to narrow them down to just one. To set the stage, you will follow the same operating principles you learned in the last chapter, along with a few new rules, to ensure that you don't default to preserving option value:

OVERCOMING FOBO WHEN MAKING HIGH-STAKES DECISIONS

KEEP AN OPEN MIND: Don't fall in love with any of the possible outcomes before you've even gotten started. If you do, you might struggle to eliminate alternatives from your opportunity set.

KNOW WHAT MATTERS: Determine what are you trying to achieve and what you consider an acceptable outcome. List your criteria and the qualities associated with that outcome.

RELY ON FACTS, NOT EMOTIONS: Compile all of the information you'll need before making a decision.

GATHER DATA FROM MULTIPLE SOURCES: Don't make a decision in a vacuum. Draw on the people around you—and perhaps those beyond your immediate circle—to get advice.

REMEMBER, YOU ARE CHOOSING THE BEST, NOT CUTTING THE WORST: Once you determine that all of your options are acceptable, your decision-making process is grounded in settling on the best option among the group. Eliminating options and mourning foregone opportunities is very difficult for people with FOBO; therefore, you should always orient your decision toward reinforcing the conviction that you are choosing wisely.

Once you have internalized these basic principles, you will proceed with the decision-making process.

Step 1: Formulate the Question

Once again, you must first articulate a question that summarizes what's giving you FOBO. Doing so is essential to framing the remainder of your decision-making process. Your goal is to state your upcoming decision clearly and concisely, along the lines of: "Which of these four cars should I buy?" or "Which of these eight candidates should I hire?"

Step 2: Set Criteria to Frame Your Decision

As before, you will set some basic parameters that will determine whether a given opportunity meets your standards. Remember, it's OK to try to maximize your outcome; you will need to determine what's important to you so that you can make a decision based on the merits. That said, it's best to avoid overcomplicating your process by setting too many criteria and risking analysis paralysis. If you cannot make a decision based on less than five or ten criteria, then you will struggle. In that case, you must pare down your list.

Step 3: Gather Data

As you conduct due diligence, you will gather information in order to verify that your assumptions about the attractiveness of each possible option are correct, just as you did in the last chapter. As you rely on facts and data to strip away information asymmetry, you will make sure that there is "enough good" in each potential decision. If something does not meet your basic criteria, you will then permanently eliminate it from consideration.

Step 4: Select an Initial Front-Runner

To get to this point, you've done a lot of research. As a result, you can trust your intuition to allow you to identify the presumptive leader of the pack from among the remaining alternatives. Since you have ensured that all of your choices are acceptable, there is no downside to identifying a favorite. You will trust your gut to select the one alternative that you believe can offer the most upside and that is the most exciting to you. This will be your benchmark—your "best option." Even if your intuition isn't perfect, you cannot lose: all of the remaining options have "enough good," so you can be comfortable that your criteria will be met.

Step 5: Systematically Eliminate Inferior Options

You will then compare each candidate to your front-runner. If a choice is not a "better option" than the front-runner, you will then pull a Marie Kondo, say "thank u, next," and eliminate it from consideration. Since eliminating options and letting go of foregone opportunities is very difficult for people with FOBO, remember at all times that by following this process you are always choosing the better of the two options before you.

You will continue this process and prune your list of alternatives by comparing each one to the front-runner. You will also give yourself the flexibility to replace your best option at any point in the process. Front-runner status is never permanent, so if you decide to replace the front-runner, then it too must be eliminated. You will repeat this process until you are left with just two options: your first-choice pick and a backup. You will only return to the backup if you find that your first choice is no longer available for some reason.

Throughout this entire process, you will stay true to one critical and unalienable tenet: once you eliminate an option, it's gone. You will not revisit it and you will no longer fear it. You risk getting mired in FOBO when you continue to return to the same alternatives over and over, so you will avoid this temptation at all costs.

Step 6: Write It Down

Just as you did in the last chapter, you will create a written memo of the rationale you used to build your case. Committing your ideas to paper will help you to ensure that your logic is well thought-out and comprehensive. You will also resist the temptation to rank your choices as you work. Instead, you will consider each option individually and then keep it on your list or eliminate it based on its own merits. The minute you start ranking your choices, you risk complicating your assessment and provoking FOBO all over again.

What If You're Still Stuck?

If you find that you cannot whittle your options down to just a few or that you cannot rank those final two choices, then you will call in the cavalry. Venture capital firms have investment committees that review each investment decision, kick the tires, ask hard questions, and then either approve or reject an investment. Getting an objective take from people who are well-informed and want the best for you can provide perspective and a final gut check before you commit to one direction or another. In assembling this group, favor diversity so that you can benefit from a range of opinions and ideas. In order to avoid unnecessary complexity, make sure to limit your committee to less than five people. Also, try to have an odd number of advisors—if it comes down to voting, you'll have a tie-breaker at the ready.

Despite the stakes at play, you can feel comfortable relying on the judgment of outsiders. Since this is FOBO, you are choosing from among multiple acceptable outcomes. You are at the point where, despite your work up to this point, the differences between your remaining options are so hard to spot that you are stuck. It's time to decide, and if you cannot do it alone, then you must ask for help. In the process, you will have the opportunity to explain how you have arrived at your final possible options. As you do so, you may face probing questions that cause you to rethink your calculations and even change your mind. That's perfectly natural. But you must weigh any new data against your original criteria. Unless there is some drastic change, new information could serve as a Trojan horse that results in procrastination and delays action.

Once you have made a decision, your work is not over. Since venture capitalists shouldn't romanticize their decisions, neither should you. Once they make a decision, lots of unexpected things can happen. They must remain engaged, attentive, and ready to deal with the consequences of their actions. In fact, every year investors look back at their portfolios and compare the performance of each company with the assumptions that they made at the time of the investment. You can follow a similar approach by revisiting your decisions from time to time and learning from them. What did you do right or wrong? Who gave you great advice and who led you astray? What would you have done differently?

When you make decisions, you accept that your choices and your logic could be proven wrong down the line. Just like investments, decisions come with risks, and you will inevitably build your own anti-portfolio of bad decisions and mistakes from which you can learn. You also recognize that what makes sense today may no longer work for you in a year. Even if you've taken the wrong path, when you're decisive, you can use the strategy outlined earlier to work through the next impasse or challenge in order to move in a new direction.

Now that you've got the tools to focus and make decisions with conviction, you are on the road to overcoming your FOs. No matter how much progress you make, however, you must stay alert. As you move through the world, there will be distractions, most of which are technological, that will tempt you and imperil your progress. That's why you will need more tools in your arsenal. The next chapter will provide you with strategies that will help you cut out the noise, focus on what matters, and miss out on the rest.

CHAPTER 12

Missing Out on the Rest

"Men must be decided on what they will not do, and then they are able to act with vigor in what they ought to do."
—MENCIUS

Once you know what you actually want, the next phase of work begins. You may have done everything you needed to do to settle on an option—just one option—and you're feeling good. You've made it. You're decisive! Rather than offer my sincere congratulations, however, I'll instead issue a warning: you're not out of the woods yet. That's because the world is constantly conspiring to convince you that you've got it all wrong. Every day, either consciously or subconsciously, you face an onslaught of ads, posts, notifications, articles, conversations, or other sources of information that offer you ready distractions from your priorities. It's overwhelming.

Even as I write this, I'm fighting the temptation to take a news break, check my texts, scroll through Twitter, or respond to that WhatsApp message that just appeared on my screen. Even as you read this, you're facing the same onslaught of stimuli. While giving in to temptation and taking a quick break may allow you to learn something latent, awaken a latent interest, or inspire some future action, the most likely result is that all of this information provokes your FOs. Your decision, which seemed so certain and well-reasoned, suddenly feels hasty. You feel a pang of doubt. Perhaps you should revisit your options once again? Despite your best efforts, you've been pulled right back into the fight for clarity now that indecision once again threatens to cloud your intuition.

Once you've chosen what you actually want, you must find the power to miss out on the rest. That is the *preventative medicine* that will allow you to thrive in a world that is constantly undermining your efforts to conquer FOMO and FOBO. When you learn to miss out, you will be able to *focus* on what matters. To best position yourself for success by cutting out the noise, there are two types of actions—both of which fall completely under your control—that will help you to focus: (i) making manageable changes to behavior and (ii) leveraging technology.

1. **Making Manageable Changes to Behavior:** You will eliminate the daily obstacles that can serve as barriers to actually sticking with the course of action you have decided to embrace. That means managing all of the factors—things like relentless access to information, reference anxiety, choice overload, and narcissism—that can lead you astray. To do so you will make pragmatic changes to behavior and mindset that will allow you to think and operate differently than you have in the past. That said, there is no point in pursuing a strategy that is not sustainable or practical for someone living in the modern world. No one expects you to be a Luddite. Every solution proposed in this book acknowledges that we live in a digital

world and that you must manage, rather than eliminate, technology in order to succeed.

2. **Leveraging Technology:** You will also think carefully—and clinically—about how you use technology. In some cases, you will eliminate or decrease your exposure to all of the noise that it generates. For example, you can choose to banish all electronics from the bedroom, remove certain apps from your devices, or institute distraction-free hours in your day. In other cases, you will embrace digital tools to make your time count for more or to repurpose it. There are a number of new technologies and applications—from meditation apps to digital wellness tools—that can free you from distractions, raise your consciousness, and return your focus. These choices and strategies will position you to find focus as you navigate your way through an overwhelming world.

The Epic Battle for Your Consciousness

The role of technology in provoking and sustaining FOMO and FOBO is clear. Persistent connectivity, internet-driven information overload, and social media have reshaped how you live your life, how you conduct business, and how you relate to your fellow *FOMO sapiens* and *FOBO sapiens*. Even if you've managed to make a decision and commit to a course of action, that stimuli will still be there. It will remind you of all the things you might be missing out on, and it will present you with an array of options that just might be better. While the internet is the conduit for many of these changes, much of the responsibility for this dynamic falls to the corporations whose products determine how you navigate the online world. The ascension of today's leading technology companies in terms of power, influence, and value cannot be under-stated. Apple, Alphabet (Google's parent company), Amazon, Tencent, Alibaba, and Facebook now regularly rank among the ten most valuable companies in the world.[1] Here's the business model that got them there: they are engineering technology that takes advantage of human psychol-ogy in order to monopolize our attention and then sell it to advertisers.

A big part of these companies' success is derived from their ability to create products that slowly creep into your daily routine and conscious-ness until you cannot live without them. They are designed to become indispensable. If you think about it, the alarm clock on your cell phone is like a Trojan horse. It's one of the reasons why people started taking their phones into the bedroom in the first place. As a result of that seemingly innocuous action, they end up checking email, news, and texts in the middle of the night. You can call these features habit-forming or you can call them addictive, but either way, they compel you to spend an inordi-nate amount of time staring at a screen.

In the early years of the internet, most people were too busy having their minds blown by all of these new, cool, and largely "free" products to worry about their long-term effects. Digital tools do something magical—they make sure that everyone who picks up their phone can feel like they live in a choice-rich environment. More recently, however, the tide has turned. People have realized that they have become so tethered to their devices that they are paying a price, in terms of their physical, mental, and emotional health.

Big tech has gotten the message. In May 2018, Google CEO Sundar Pichai took the stage at Google I/O, the company's developer summit, to declare that going forward, Google would infuse "digital wellbeing" into its suite of products.[2] In his comments, he explicitly confronted his company's contribution to stoking the collective FOMO, stating:

Based on our research, we know that people feel tethered to their devices… There is increasing social pressure to respond to anything you get right away. People are anxious to stay up to date with all of the information out there. They have FOMO, Fear of Missing Out. We think there's a chance for us to do better.

Pichai then announced a new mindset that will course through every platform at Google. It will include tools that monitor your time spent online, analyze your behavior, help you to understand your habits, and then enable you to switch off. Just a few weeks later, Apple announced its own suite of digital wellness features, including enhanced Do Not Disturb, changes to notifications, and reporting about how much time you're spending on your device. While these tools are focused on addressing FOMO, technology can be just as powerful in stoking FOBO. After all, overwhelming information and abundant choice, both of which are core to the business models of most technology companies, are two of its most potent drivers. Thus, while Google and Apple haven't mentioned FOBO quite yet, I expect they may well do so in the future.

Even though they have decided to offer you tools to manage your interactions with their products, Apple and Google continue to create highly addictive digital products. So do Facebook, Pinterest, LinkedIn, and the thousands of companies of all shapes and sizes that seek to carve out a little bit (or a lot) of your brain for themselves. If you hope to escape unscathed from the war for your attention, I have bad news for you. These companies are engaging in an epic and persistent battle to keep you using their products. They have tools—in the form of artificial intelligence, predictive analytics, and viral marketing campaigns—that are specifically designed to wear you down and monopolize a growing share of your mind. It's almost like they are bringing a pistol, or many pistols, to a knife fight. You never stood a chance.

These companies know exactly what they're doing. That's why it's not surprising that the very people who are designing these products are in a panic about how *screen time* will affect their own families. Case in point: tech executives are increasingly imposing strict no-screen policies on their children. Some now require their nannies to sign draconian contracts prohibiting the use of devices around the kids.[3] In Silicon Valley, things are so out of hand that self-appointed tech vigilantes have been known to spy on caretakers. These Dirty Harrys and Harriets take photos of nannies using their devices in public and post them to local parenting message boards. The fever pitch tells you all you need to know about what Silicon Valley thinks of the health effects of its products. *If a chef won't eat his own cooking, you might want to move on to the next restaurant.*

As the negative effects of social media and information overload become apparent, a backlash has begun, with industry leaders calling for a radical rethinking of how we stay connected. At the 2018 World Economic Forum in Davos, Salesforce CEO Marc Benioff even suggested that governments should regulate social media platforms "exactly the same way that you regulated the cigarette industry."[4] That's why, in the absence of such regulation, the technology industry has decided to begin regulating itself. Of course, when an industry babysits itself, it does so with a specific set of objectives and incentives in mind. If you view these efforts charitably, you believe that these companies' competitive advantage in the future will be derived from how effectively they support the health and wellness of their consumers today. If you are a skeptic, then you see these efforts was a way to use digital wellness as a branding tool.

If you want to see the power that technology exerts on your daily life, you can easily take a pulse by undertaking a digital audit in order to better understand how you're engaging with all of the forces that compete for your attention. As you do so, you can use one of the many apps or digital wellness features (such as those embedded in Apple and Android products) that will help you track your time both online and on your devices.

Who's Winning the Battle for Your Consciousness?

Consider each of the questions below and take note of the answers.

INTERNET AND SOCIAL MEDIA USAGE

1. How much time do you spend online on a typical day?
2. How much time do you spend on social media on a typical day?
3. How many times do you check each of these sites and apps per day? How much time do you spend on them?

WhatsApp

Facebook

Instagram

Twitter

LinkedIn

Snapchat

YouTube

Wikipedia

Google and other search engines

Amazon

Reddit

Netflix

News sites (i.e., New York Times, CNN, Yahoo! News, Huffington Post, Google, Fox News)

Other (i.e., games, dating apps, podcasts, streaming music, etc.)

4. How often do you post to social media sites?

5. Do you keep track of how many likes you or others receive on social media posts?

6. Do you judge the quality of a post based on the number of likes it received?

DIGITAL AND INFORMATION OVERLOAD

1. How many times per day do you check television or the internet for breaking news?

2. How often do you check email?

3. Do you have notifications enabled to alert you when you receive new messages or emails?

4. When you receive a notification, do you act upon it immediately?

5. When is the last time you have gone more than twelve hours without checking email or social media?

6. Do you feel stress when you are separated from your digital devices?

7. Do you feel a sense of relief when you check your email, messages, or social media accounts?

8. When you are standing in line or waiting for someone, do you spend that period online?

RELATIONSHIP WITH DEVICES

1. How much time do you spend on your devices per day?

2. How many times do you pick up your devices per day?

3. Do you keep your phone near your bed when you're sleeping?

4. Do you check your phone immediately upon waking up in the morning?

5. Do you check your phone immediately before going to sleep at night?

6. Do you frequently surf the web or use social media apps while watching television?

7. Do you keep your phone on the table during meetings or meals?

8. Do you check your phone during conversations?

9. Are you often distracted during conference calls or meetings because you're online?

10. Do family or friends complain that you spend too much time on your phone?

There are no "right" or "wrong" answers to the questions above. Depending on what you do for a living or where you are in your life, you may engage more or less with the internet and with your devices. But regardless of how you spend your days, you need to be aware of how digital devices are shaping them. If you look at your results and find that you are surprised (I was), disturbed (I was), or even a little depressed (I was) at what you discover about yourself, then you're not alone. Smartphone addiction has become widespread, particularly among younger users, to the point that two of Apple's major investors issued a public letter that called upon the company to take steps to address this risk (and likely helped to spur the company's digital wellness drive).

Of course, that doesn't mean that technology is "bad." The internet, and in particular social media, contributes plenty of valuable things to your life and to society as a whole. Thanks to these products, you can connect with friends, meet new people, find a romantic partner, spark a revolution, and raise awareness of critical issues that would never get the media's attention otherwise. Still, whether it's trolling for breaking news, spending hours with your earbuds firmly in place, or burying your nose in a phone all day, these distractions are systematically taking over your life and undermining all of your efforts to be decisive. In the process, the constant distraction keeps you from living in the present, enjoying the moment, and engaging with the world around you. You also become increasingly isolated from your family, your friends, and all of those random people whose paths you cross on a daily basis without even noticing. Worst of all, you stop paying attention to yourself and to what you actually want to do with your life.

Putting Technology in Its Place

Stressed and distracted, people are looking for answers in the form of meditation, yoga classes, and apps that will monitor or limit their screen time. Soon they will be the first generation of guinea pigs for digital wellness initiatives crafted by untold numbers of technology companies. These companies are making mindfulness a billion-dollar industry that's only going to grow from here.[5] With so much money at stake, the war for your attention has barely begun. We have only seen the opening salvo in what promises to be a long, drawn-out series of skirmishes, fueled by technology, money, and a collective realization that the current trajectory of our connectivity is unsustainable.

Addressing your screen-related ailments though digital wellness initiatives is certainly a good first step to taking back some autonomy. At the same time, most of these tools and apps are nothing more than bandages. You can do as many digital detoxes as you want, but at some point, you're going to have to pick up your phone and use it. If you live and work in modern society, there is no all-or-nothing option for tech in your life, so you've got to find the right balance.

The benefits of rethinking and reframing your relationship with your devices and all of the programs and apps that run on them are clear. In the study "No More FOMO: Limiting Social Media Decreases Loneliness and Depression," researchers at the University of Pennsylvania found that cutting back on the use of social media sites such as Facebook, Snapchat, and Instagram lowered rates of FOMO, anxiety, depression, and loneliness among a group of undergraduate students. The researcher who designed the study specifically opted to have the students continue using social media, but with limits, as she viewed a complete detox as an "unrealistic goal."[6]

She's right. If you want to limit the role of technology in driving your FOs, you have to be realistic: *The goal isn't abstinence, it's control.* One approach to employ this mindset is to think of limiting technology like a diet. If you want to stay healthy and look good, you clearly shouldn't graze on snacks all day. If you want to stay mentally healthy and on top of your game, you must avoid snacking digitally as well. Email, texting, social media, notifications, and all of the other little snacks on your phone will weigh you down if you consume them all the time. By limiting snacks to a few times a day, however, you can stay mentally fit while avoiding the need to go cold turkey and disengage completely (which is basically impossible). That includes implementing small but important steps like disabling notifications, tracking screen time, erasing distraction-causing apps from your phone, and taking breaks from your devices altogether to allow for focused work or social activities. Just like when you cut out junk food from your diet, you'll soon realize that you feel a lot better when you're free from the constant interruptions.

You'll also discover that there are very few matters in life that need your immediate attention. It's logical to be concerned that by cutting notifications and disconnecting from "always on" mode, you will miss something important. There is a risk, a very small yet psychologically important probability, that you will miss a life-altering phone call or a transformational bit of news. There's also a chance that when you leave your house on a given day you will trip and injure yourself, get mugged, or be struck by lightning. Still, you accept that liability, open the door, and go out into the world regardless. That is the price of freedom. The same applies to technology. In order to take back power from your devices, you will have to run the risk that you will miss out on something. Of course, if someone urgently needs to reach you, they will find a way to do so, just as our ancestors did in the technological dark ages.

Putting technology in its place isn't just a theoretical construct, it's also very much about how you coexist with technology and your devices in the physical world. A recent survey by Asurion found that 70 percent of all adults and 88 percent of millennials sleep with their phones within reach.[7] Whenever I hear statistics like that, I wonder what I would have thought of that as a kid. Would I have been amazed or horrified to think that in the future most people would spend nearly all of their time with a computer at arm's length? The creep of technology into formerly tech-free places like the bedroom is astounding, but you don't have to take it lying down.

Arianna Huffington came up with an innovative solution to the encroachment of technology on your personal space. Huffington is the founder of Thrive Global, a firm that is combatting the "delusion that burnout is the price we must pay for success." She's also an expert on the science of sleep. If you've ever heard her speak, she'll likely tell you how she's managed to help people solve their tech addiction and their sleep problems with one clever product. To make sure your devices don't trump your wellness, she has invented a phone "bed" that becomes part of your nighttime routine. You can literally tuck in your phone, plug it in for charging, and then say goodbye until morning, when you'll meet again, both recharged and ready for the day ahead. I firmly agree with Huffington. The bedroom should be a phone-free zone, and that's long been my own policy, although I have to admit that my iPhone prefers to sleep naked on the kitchen counter.

Digital Mindfulness or Just Mindfulness?

Even as digital wellness and digital mindfulness have become buzzwords over the past few years, so has mindfulness, plain and simple. This is a positive development. While technology enables distraction, humans have struggled with the FOs for time immemorial. As a result, you'll need to address more than your technology issues if you're going to prevail. Perhaps that's why practices like meditation are no longer just for people living on the fringe. Today, you can take your pick of apps like Headspace and Ten Percent Happier or take a meditation class if you want to give it a try. If you're just getting going with mindfulness, it's natural to think that these practices are somehow new or that they have been evolving to reflect the pressures of living in an always-on society. You'd be wrong.

Michael Rogan is a neuroscientist and psychotherapist who got a PhD at New York University (NYU) and did his post-doctoral work at Columbia University. He's also been practicing Buddhist meditation for over forty years. Given these three areas of expertise, Rogan has built his career at the crossroads of contemporary psychology, behavioral neuro-science, and the ancient practices of Buddhism. It turns out that things haven't changed as much as you would think since 500 BCE. Buddhist meditation has been around for over 2,500 years, because even in the time of Buddha, people struggled with anxiety and stress just as they do today. They still felt FOMO and FOBO, although the triggers were different. Buddhism even has its own word—*dukkha*, or "pervasive dissatisfaction"—for these types of feelings.[8]

While there are many psychological techniques to address your FOs, Rogan suggests that one of the most straightforward is mindfulness. In fact, the practices that were originated by Buddha and his adherents have now been accepted as treatment protocols by modern-day therapists. Here's how it works. When you practice mindfulness, you intentionally place your attention on your physical presence. You pay attention to the chair on which you're sitting, notice how your body feels, observe the sensations of the breath, and take note of the sounds around you. When you direct your attention in this way, you do something important—you disrupt your habitual thinking about the future, the past, or what you're missing. You also leave behind your wants, needs, desires, and insecurities. You are present in the moment.

Being present is the opposite of FOMO and FOBO. When you are consumed by your FOs, you forget about all of the other things that are happening around you at that very moment. You forget that the sky is blue or that it's cold outside. You forget to be present. That's the secret sauce of mindfulness. When you're noticing what you're feeling at that moment, say while taking a breath, you're not thinking about the past or the future. After all, you cannot feel a breath that you took five minutes ago or a breath you will take in an hour. If you are noticing your breath as you take it, however, you are assured to be present, because you can only feel that sensation at that exact moment.

One of the important things you learn from this experience is that you have a choice as to how you direct your mind and energy. If you want to focus on now and leave yesterday and tomorrow alone, you can do so, at least for a few minutes, so that you can give your mind a break from the habitual churning that occupies it all day long. In fact, as you practice more, you realize that you can make the choice to break away whenever you want, at least for a few moments or minutes. You have agency in your life, and you can choose where to place your attention. You can take a much-needed break from all of the traps that you encounter every day. As you do so, it is important to make time each and every day for this exercise. That's not a new rule promoted by a bunch of trendy meditation apps; it's a long-standing best practice that you too should embrace.

You may have heard about mindfulness but thought that was just a bit too "woo-woo" for you. The concept can conjure up images of New Agey things like crystals, turquoise jewelry, and kombucha, and it's easy to lump them all together and dismiss mindfulness as well. It's worth reconsidering this preconception, especially when you consider how many businesspeople—folks such as Oprah, Marc Benioff, and Ray Dalio—use these practices to reduce stress, improve mental clarity, and exert greater emotional control. Meditation and mindfulness don't have to be New Agey unless you want them to be. Instead, you can think of them as another string in your bow that will help you to perform your best and stay resilient in challenging times.

Even if the idea of mindfulness makes sense to you and you've wanted to integrate this kind of activity into your life, doing so is easier said than done for many people. It's not that it's hard, per se, it's just that it's hard to make it a priority. Take it from me. I've spent years trying to meditate. I've downloaded apps, taken classes, you name it. Yet while I've been able to keep things up for a few days here and there, I've struggled to create any sort of habit or routine. I always get too busy or too distracted to remember to meditate every day.

When I expressed that frustration to Dr. Rogan, he encouraged me to rethink how I see mindfulness. He suggests that the best way to integrate this practice into your life is to remember that being mindful doesn't *have* to take the form of sitting still. There is a popular perception that unless you sit on the floor cross-legged and chant, or go on a fourteen-day retreat to Thailand, you're not doing it right. That is a myth. There's a reason why lots of people have their best ideas in the shower. It's because, for that brief period of time, you are likely being mindful, even if you didn't realize it. As the water hits you, you're noticing it. You are present and as a result, good things happen. In the same vein, washing the dishes or laying on your couch with your dog could be an effective way to be present.

Bear in mind that this is not supposed to be hard. If you think it's hard and you feel like you have to exert force on your mind to make progress, then you're missing the point. *Your goal is to give your mind a break, not work it harder.* If you find it to be a struggle, don't worry. Like most other things in life, you're probably going to need to practice. As you do, you can always seek out guidance, in the form of a class or a teacher, to help you along your way.

Mindfulness can also take unexpected forms that tie to other important parts of your life. Monsignor Dolan, whom you met earlier, believes that the key to overcoming FOMO and FOBO is to find time for contemplation, meditation, and reflection. For him and many others, this takes the form of prayer. You can also apply similar principles to exercise, walking around your city or town, or even listening to music. When it comes to any of these activities, the key is to place your attention on something that you normally don't even notice and that is happening at that very moment. It could take the form of observing the beat of a song or the feeling of your feet hitting the ground as you walk or run.

You can also use—gasp—technology to help you. In my own struggles to begin a meditation practice, I've used two apps that have made a big difference. First, I downloaded Oak, which offers a cool (and free) way to time your meditation sessions. While that was a good start, I still found that I couldn't sustain a meditation practice beyond a few days, usually when I was traveling and faced few of the distractions of home. Thankfully, my friend Ajay Kishore was feeling much the same. An entrepreneur who was in the middle of fundraising, he was also looking for a way to cut stress and escape the FOs that are inherent in raising capital.

Ajay and I decided to use the app HabitShare to keep each other honest about our daily meditation practice. Each day, we check in to affirm that we have, in fact, meditated. When one of us misses a day or two, we keep each other honest. When I failed to check in for a few days while on vacation in Paris, he sent me the following text: "Red wine and people watching isn't a replacement." Sometimes shaming people works; I made time to meditate during the remainder of the trip. Thanks to these small changes in behavior, enhanced with a little technology, for the first time in my life, I have stuck to meditation for over a year and have begun to see its benefits. Do I see the irony in using two apps and setting up a competitive accountability system to get me to meditate? Definitely. But if that's what it takes to get into a routine, then I say no judgment. To me, these apps serve as antibodies against the infection that is created by all the other apps on my phone.

It would be impossible to explore digital wellness and mindfulness fully on these pages, since the subject is vast. Luckily, it's a topic that has attracted increasing attention, and there are many terrific resources available at your local bookstore or online if you want to learn more.

Just remember, as you contemplate your relationship with technology and explore different ways to miss out, always keep the following basic precepts in mind:

1. The goal isn't abstinence; it's control.

2. Find ways to free yourself from "always on" mode.

3. Put technology in its place.

4. Make time for mindfulness, in whatever form that takes for you.

The Joy of Missing Out

In the very same keynote at Google I/O, Sundar Pichai also dropped another four-letter word that he declared to be the antidote to FOMO:

> People are anxious to stay up to date with all of the information out there. They have FOMO, Fear of Missing Out. We think there's a chance for us to do better. We've been talking to people and some people introduced to us the concept of JOMO, the actual Joy of Missing Out. So, we think we can really help users with digital well-being.[9]

JOMO was coined by the blogger and entrepreneur Anil Dash, whose discovery of the concept was based on the insight that "when you get old and wonderfully, contentedly boring like me, you stay home because you'd rather be there for bath time [sic] and bedtime with the baby than, well, anywhere else in the world."[10] Since that time,

JOMO has become well-known as the catchall solution to FOMO. It has popped up in advertising campaigns, magazine articles, and all over social media. It has also followed in FOMO's footsteps to become a meme in its own right.

So, is JOMO truly the antidote to FOMO? The answer, I'd say, is *sometimes*, but certainly not always. JOMO is not a process—it's a goal. It's not the journey, it's the destination. In fact, even if you are able to get yourself into a state of full-blown JOMO, I'd argue that you're still only part of the way to getting over FOMO. The mere fact that you have to proclaim to the world that you are feeling happy because you are missing out on this thing or that strikes me as a little bit self-conscious. If you truly didn't mind missing out, it wouldn't have occurred to you to label your joy in the first place. If you're Instagraming about your JOMO, you're doing the same thing you would do if you broke up with your partner and then posted photos of you having the "best time ever!" all over the app.

So what does JOMO look like? You can get there if you have eliminated as much of the information asymmetry that drives FOMO as possible. If you generally know what you're missing and you still don't care, then you're there. Absent that clarity, it gets tougher. How can you feel JOMO if you have no idea what you're passing up? By definition, you can't be happy to miss out on something if you don't even know it exists. If that were the case, everyone would be in a permanent state of JOMO because of the millions of events happening around the world that they never even knew were taking place. Further, JOMO works best when it comes to the smaller things in life. Missing out on a social event, a weekend trip, or some other type of ephemeral commitment can indeed feel good. But nobody is going to run around exclaiming that they're feeling JOMO about finding true love, building a rewarding career, or starting an entrepreneurial or nonprofit venture. You can definitely have lots of FOMO about those things, but you'll never feel JOMO.

If JOMO isn't going to save you when it comes to some of the dreams you've long harbored or adventures you wish you could pursue, you're going to need to find another way. Luckily, it's possible to pay attention to your FOMO, learn from it, and then turn it into a force for good. In the next section of the book, you will discover how to repurpose FOMO to make it work for you. You will also learn how to deal with FOMO and FOBO in others and then use them to your advantage.

SECTION IV

MAKING FOMO AND FOBO WORK FOR YOU

"It is our choices, Harry, that show what we truly are, far more than our abilities."

—HARRY POTTER AND THE CHAMBER OF SECRETS

CHAPTER 13

Going All In Some of the Time

"I see some people stay in one place because it's convenient or it's comfortable. But they're missing out on their passion."
—ARIANNA HUFFINGTON

Florencia Jimenez-Marcos lives in Miami Beach with her husband Xavier Gonzalez-Sanfeliu and their daughter, Cecilia. A ball of energy who is highly engaged with the world around her, Florencia is the kind of person I'd classify as high-risk when it comes to FOMO. Although she's ambitious and always up for an adventure, she isn't prone to taking actions that will unnecessarily complicate her family's vibrant and busy life. While Florencia loves her current existence, she also knows that she could have ended up building a life in many other places. She could have moved back to her native Argentina, returned to Houston where she grew up, leveraged her fluent French to live in Paris, or joined Xavier in New York. Instead, she and Xavier chose each other and Miami, and after nearly two decades in the city, the family is rooted there.

Except for a few months every year when they're not. Florencia and Xavier have created jobs that can travel with them, so every summer, they embark on what Florencia calls a "mini-life." As soon as school finishes for Cecilia, they pack their bags and head off to some far-flung part of the world. It's not an extended vacation, but rather a way to live and work in a new place.

Their goal is to experience a different, parallel life and return home having grown in some way.

By finding like-minded families who are willing to exchange homes, they have spent time in Singapore, Indonesia, Spain, Canada, Holland, England, and France. With each new country, they learn something new, thrive as a family, and scratch the itch of "What if?" Then they return to Miami, grateful to be home and with their FOMO firmly under control.

Good FOMO versus Bad FOMO

Even when you live with conviction, that doesn't mean that you should never look back and wonder about what might have been. It's natural to contemplate the paths and choices that you have to discard if you're going to be decisive. As a native New Englander, I've long loved the Robert Frost classic "The Road Not Taken":

> *Two roads diverged in a wood, and I—*
> *I took the one less traveled by,*
> *And that has made all the difference.*

It's a romantic notion, the kind of poem that is solemnly read out at graduation ceremonies in order to encourage people to follow their dreams, do something different, and stay far away from the herd of wildebeests. It's also not particularly practical. Lots of people cannot afford to take the road less traveled. They have bills to pay and responsibilities to shoulder, or they're simply afraid to leave the manicured path for the wilds that lie beyond their field of vision. Even Frost himself protested that his poem was misunderstood. In a letter to a friend, he lamented that the piece was "taken pretty seriously…despite doing my best to make it obvious by my manner that I was fooling… Mea culpa."[1] Funny, I wonder why no one ever reads that last bit at commencement.

When you are decisive, you say no to many things. Once you learn to control FOMO, you accept that you simply cannot do *everything*—that's the point of having focus. And that means that you will *miss out* on certain experiences. Despite your best efforts, you may struggle with indecision along the way. It's important to remember that not all FOMO is bad. You can actually learn a lot from FOMO if you listen to it. After all, it's constantly whispering in your ear to provide you with ideas and inspiration. Most of the time, it's going to serve as little more than a distraction, but that's not always the case.

If you find yourself feeling persistent FOMO with regard to the same opportunity or decision, perhaps you should listen to that little voice in your head, the one that asks, "What if?" Your intuition might be telling you something important: You should open your eyes, look around at your surroundings, and try something new. Tackle a new goal, take a new step, and break the routine! That's easier said than done if you've already got a life full of commitments, but there is a way to channel your FOMO for good. You can wander down the path you didn't choose without upsetting the one that you did. For example, you can embark on a mini-life like Florencia, changing up your surroundings every once in a while. You can also stop dismissing possibilities out of hand before trying to think differently about how you might actually make them happen. Whatever you choose to do, your goal is to figure out how you can make FOMO work for you so that life isn't quite so black-and-white and cut-and-dried—it can be far more nuanced.

The secret to harnessing FOMO and reframing it for good comes down to how you decide to act. Whether you are exploring new adventures, building a business, or trying to change the world, you don't have to go all in. Instead, you can *go all in some of the time.* That's a form of conscious multitasking that I first applied to the world of entrepreneurship. I have since extended this approach to other endeavors that stretch far beyond the world of business. This allows you to challenge yourself and your perception of what is possible without radically changing the rest of your life or going broke. Ironically, the same forces that provoke FOMO in many people—ubiquitous access to information and extreme interconnectivity caused by technology—are part of what makes this strategy possible.

Becoming an Entrepreneur While Keeping Your Day Job

There's never been a better time to be an entrepreneur. Consider the extent to which technology is now woven into the fabric of our personal and professional lives. This is a game changer for anyone who wants to start a new venture, since you can operate with far more flexibility than in the past. For the first time in history, you can work on whatever you want at the time and the place of your choosing. All you need is an internet connection, a smartphone, and perhaps a laptop, and you're in business. Plus, many of the critical resources you will need to get started are available for free or at a minimal cost. As a result, it's never been cheaper or easier to start and manage a company.

That's why it's started to feel like just about everybody has become an entrepreneur. Shows like *Shark Tank* and *Silicon Valley* glamorize entrepreneurship while the media lionizes start-up founders, especially the ones who have made it big. Meanwhile, companies like WeWork are riding the entrepreneurship wave by trying to convince everyone to start a company and chase after their dreams. The company's motto, "Do What You Love," makes it clear: the path to self-actualization runs right through the office that you are going to rent from WeWork when you get the courage to start your own company. These messages are highly aspirational, and they are carried with great enthusiasm by the herd. As a result, millions of people now feel entrepreneurship FOMO.

Behind all the FOMO, however, there are cold, hard facts. While the barriers to entry to entrepreneurship have fallen substantially, that doesn't mean that success has gotten any easier. Most new ventures fail. Given those odds, if you have bills to pay, quitting your day job to launch a start-up is risky at best and reckless at worst. If you are afraid of failure—and let's face it, you should be—you can fall victim to FOBO. Rather than coming up with an idea and getting started, it's tempting to sit on the sidelines and ruminate until you find the perfect business model. The problem is that if you do so, you'll be sitting on the sidelines forever. There *is* no perfect business model. Even if there were one, you probably wouldn't know it for the first few years.

Just because you take the road more traveled and pursue a traditional career doesn't mean that your choice is irrevocable. Sure, full-time entrepreneurship is a terrific path for some, but it's not for everyone. That doesn't mean you have to watch from the sidelines, feeling like everyone else is doing something exciting while you're stuck in the drudgery of your day job. Instead, you can face your FOMO head-on and wrestle it back into control by using it to your advantage. The key is to no longer think of entrepreneurship as an all-or-nothing proposition. Instead, you can become an entrepreneur while keeping your day job and combine the best of both worlds. It's a simple yet somewhat radical idea: you don't have to be an entrepreneur, but you can be *entrepreneurial*. This approach allows you to think like an owner rather than an employee. You can then embrace risk and creativity from the security of your day job. You do this by investing at least ten percent of your time, and if possible, your capital, to get involved in one or more new ventures as either a founder, an investor, or an advisor.

I call this 10% Entrepreneurship, and it was the subject of my first book, *The 10% Entrepreneur*. Since I first wrote about this concept a few years back, 10% Entrepreneurship, or what some people call side hustles, has become mainstream. I've also had the privilege of meeting hundreds of 10% Entrepreneurs in my travels, and I've been amazed at what people can accomplish when they focus, even on a part-time basis. Some of these part-timers are so successful that they are eventually able to go full-time if they so desire. They are not alone. Over the past few years, it's been amazing to witness the rise of part-time entrepreneurship more generally. In a world of increasing labor flexibility, more than 44 million Americans now have side hustles of one kind or another. It's important to remember, however, that not all side hustles are created equal. If you're driving an Uber or renting out your apartment on Airbnb, you most definitely have a side hustle, but that is not the same as 10% Entrepreneurship. The difference has to do with ownership.

Whenever a Silicon Valley start-up goes public, there are always lots of stories about the rank-and-file employees who become millionaires overnight. None of these people got rich on their salaries; they made their money from the shares that they owned in the company. Getting paid a salary is terrific—and obviously very necessary—but the real money is made when you are able to participate in the value that is created as a company grows. When you're a 10% Entrepreneur, your overarching goal is ownership. You want to own a *stake* in everything you create with the idea that your stake can grow and become far more valuable. You see your efforts as an investment rather than simply as a way to make extra money. You're not billing by the hour, but instead creating something that will be shaped by you, will belong to you, and will be built on terms that are set by you.

Take the case of Matipa, Mercy, and Maona Nyamangwanda, who are the creators of EnnyEthnic, a fashion line that uses heritage African prints to celebrate the sisters' Zimbabwean heritage. Although they have long dreamed of starting an apparel business, as recent immigrants to the United States, the sisters sought to build stable careers first. Matipa works as a lawyer for the U.S. government and Mercy is a nurse, while Maona owns a cleaning business.

In order to combine the stability of their careers with the excitement and upside of entrepreneurship, the sisters decided to launch EnnyEthnic as a part-time e-commerce venture while keeping their day jobs. This has allowed them to grow their business without having to worry about how they are going to pay the bills. It also allows them to combine their love for their homeland with an opportunity to build financial independence. Their approach has worked: the company was featured at San Francisco Fashion Week, opened pop-up shops on both the East and West Coasts of the United States, and even had a runway show at Milan Fashion Week! While the sisters might consider going full-time in the future, launching the business part-time has allowed them to pursue their dream without risking their lifestyles or their sanity to do so.

If you don't yet have an idea or you aren't prepared for the responsibility of running your own venture, you can still be a part-time entrepreneur. Rather than starting and running your own business, you can invest your time or capital in other people's projects. That's how I ended up as a shareholder in more than twenty ventures. Two of these companies are now unicorns, meaning that they are worth at least one billion dollars, and the growth in the value of my investments in those companies far outstrips any return I could have gotten in the stock market. It's sort of mind-blowing.

How Part-Time Entrepreneurship Spurs Innovation

On the surface, engaging in ventures outside of your day job can seem rooted in self-interest. You are using your skills, your network, and your knowledge, some of which you acquired at your full-time job, to create more opportunities for yourself. Yet by taking on this challenge, you are developing and deepening a series of skills and relationships and flexing a different set of muscles that will make you more effective at the office. As a result, becoming a part-time entrepreneur not only benefits you, it also benefits your employer. Everyone wins.

This mindset isn't just for individuals; companies can also manage their FOMO by taking on side projects. The term *intrapreneurship*—which describes efforts at creating a corporate culture that encourages entrepreneurial thinkers—was first coined nearly a quarter century ago. All these years later, building a truly entrepreneurial culture at a large company remains challenging, but it's not impossible.

For example, Google asks employees to spend a portion of their time focused on side projects. You can thank that program for your Gmail account. While this approach has long been fundamental to new product development, it now serves an additional purpose: Google is no longer a start-up and most of its employees have not worked in a start-up environment. By baking entrepreneurship into its corporate culture, Google makes sure that every employee has authentic entrepreneurial experiences that inform the entirety of their work at the company. For every company like Google, however, there are countless other firms that have been unable to spur innovation among their ranks. Sometimes it's an issue of commitment. New ideas take time to pay off, so success or failure may come down to a company's willingness to stick with it. At a time when managers and shareholders are clamoring for short-term results, the long-term nature of intrapreneurship can make it an easy target when it comes time to cut costs or reset priorities.

Companies can take things to the next level by encouraging their employees to explore their own entrepreneurial projects and then asking them to apply what they learn back at their day jobs. In doing so, the leaders of these firms would be sending a clear message about what kind of organization they're running. Companies that leverage their employees to become leaner, faster, and more innovative are confident that they can attract and motivate talent. Perhaps most importantly, they realize that encouraging their employees to spend time on projects that interest them in their free time will serve as an important retention tool. They also recognize that if an employee dreams of leaving someday to start his own company, he's better off doing that then staying put and working half-heartedly in his current position.

Embracing Activism without Going Broke

While becoming an entrepreneur outside of your day job has clear implications for managing FOMO in your professional life, you can apply the same mindset to your personal life as well. The same set of factors that make it so inexpensive and accessible to become an entrepreneur today

are also relevant to nonprofits and politics. This is particularly important if your FOMO has life-altering implications, the personal stakes are
high, and you fear that you will miss out on the chance to make a difference to someone in need. But even if you're trying to change the world,
you might not be able to drop everything and charge ahead full steam.
You need to find another way—a sustainable approach—to make things
happen, and you want to be a protagonist—very much an owner—of
the endeavor. This is about more than volunteering—it's about having a
stake and a seat at the table to make sure that things get done.

Dan Brendtro's introduction to Friedreich's ataxia (FA) came four
years ago when a genetic test confirmed it as the cause of his daughter Raena's balance and coordination issues. Within a few weeks, the
family was on a plane from their home in Sioux Falls, South Dakota, to
the Children's Hospital of Philadelphia to meet with one of the world's
leading FA researchers. In their meeting, the Brendtros discovered that
the disease has no cure. It's very rare, it's very aggressive, and it typically
places a child into a wheelchair before the end of high school. FA is also
associated with early mortality and can take the lives of patients when
they are in their twenties or thirties. Although they were devastated, the
Brendtros had a reason to hope: a small but growing cadre of researchers
were working toward a cure. Critically, unlike many other rare diseases,
the biological mechanism behind FA had already been identified.

As Yael Melamed also realized when she received her cancer diagnosis, when you face a crisis, you either collapse or you take action. The
Brendtros chose to fight. When Dan approached a hospital system in
Sioux Falls in hopes of prompting new research, he encountered an
incredible coincidence: Dr. Peter Vitiello, working just four miles from
Dan's office, had briefly conducted critical research on FA a few years
prior, but the project was mothballed when funding ran out. Dan asked

how much it would cost to resume the research, and then resolved to raise enough money to make it happen. Knowing that applying for grants or other funding could take years, he understood he needed to think creatively to shorten that timeline.

Dan resolved to think like an entrepreneur, albeit on a part-time basis, to gather the funds via a crowdfunding campaign. Having read *The 10% Entrepreneur*, he dubbed this approach the 10% Activist. To achieve his objective with a manageable investment of time and a minimal investment of money, he created a nonprofit called The Finish Line Fund and drew upon people in his network to design a logo and shoot a video. He also called on the expertise of Diego Saez-Gil, a travel entrepreneur whose successful crowdfunding efforts he had read about in *The 10% Entrepreneur*. Finally, he launched a crowdfunding campaign just before Giving Tuesday, and in a matter of weeks, he raised over $125,000. Research began almost immediately, and important initial findings came in less than a year. Once The Finish Line Fund secured additional funding to become self-sustaining, Dan set his sights on new projects as a 10% Activist. His work continues with a singular goal: to move the cure for his daughter's rare disease ever closer to the finish line.

By becoming a 10% Activist, Dan's approach was rooted in the lesson that legions of 10% Entrepreneurs have learned for themselves: whether you are trying to explore new adventures, build a business, or change the world, you don't have to go all in. Instead, you can *go all in some of the time*. This strategy allows you to manage your FOs, challenge your perception of what is possible, and have a *stake* in the outcome, without radically changing the rest of your life or endangering your finances.

Going All In Some of the Time to Achieve Goals or Explore Passions

In 2016, nine of the ten most watched television programs in the UK were episodes of the phenomenon known as the *Great British Bake Off (GBBO)*. If you haven't seen it, *GBBO* is a reality show in which Britain's top amateur bakers gather in a tent in the English countryside. They spend the next two days competing in a series of challenges, like making twenty-four identical poppy seed scones or constructing a multi-level wedding cake. Since it's the UK, everyone is terribly nice to each other, highly self-critical, and tries to keep a stiff upper lip, no matter how badly things go in the kitchen. Even the prize for winning the entire competition, a cake stand and some flowers, is classic British understatement.

Building on its success in the UK, the show has gone on to become a worldwide hit. Part of its appeal lies in its unfailing niceness. In a complicated and overwhelming world, watching people agonize over how long to bake biscotti in hopes of winning a cake stand is surprisingly comforting. I don't even like baking, but I credit *GBBO* with getting me through writer's block on a number of occasions while writing this very book. Beyond its therapeutic effects, however, the appeal of the show is also rooted in wish fulfillment. We all have hobbies that we would love to pursue professionally, and we all have secret talents that, if nurtured, could actually allow us to do so. Many of us do explore those passions, via a cooking class here or a 5K there, but the stakes are very low. That's what makes *GBBO* special. The official prize may be negligible, but the stakes are exceedingly high. Millions of people are watching each week, and the top performers might just leverage their new-found fame to launch a part-time or even a full-time career centered around baking, as many past contestants have done. Just like a part-time entrepreneur or activist, they have a *stake* in what they're building.

While part-time entrepreneurship and activism are great for exploring a professional or personal objective and tackling your FOMO, you can apply this mindset more broadly, even to baking! While lots of people would love to move to Paris for a few years and learn French, sadly that's not realistic for most people. Instead, you can use conscious multitasking to learn French. When they want to learn a language, lots of people take a class in their community or study online. That's a great start, but you can also find other ways to *go all in some of the time*, to immerse yourself in the language as much as possible. This could include getting your news each day from a French-language podcast, following all the French newspapers on Twitter, or seeking out French speakers and practicing with them.

The fundamental element that makes all of this work—and this is critical to anything you seek to achieve through an incremental approach—is that your efforts will be sustainable. Nothing about maintaining these habits feels hard. You're not making major sacrifices since you're integrating your new passion into your daily life in a way that fits comfortably and is entirely pragmatic. You can also take things to the next level so that you have a *stake*—a purpose—for continuing to improve. This could include taking a vacation in a French-speaking country or signing up for a project at work that will allow you to use your new skills. No matter what you choose, your efforts will have spillover effects into the rest of your life. Knowing that you will be putting your skills to the test for some greater benefit will allow you to challenge and even surprise yourself in the process.

Whether you're interested in cooking, learning a new language, improving your fitness, or exploring entrepreneurship or social causes, you can integrate lots of activities into your life and harness your FOMO without upsetting your routine or sacrificing everything else you're doing. When you pursue these endeavors by *going all in some of the time,* you can explore your passions and interests sustainably and set yourself up for success and fulfillment. At the same time, you can begin to set higher goals, create some stakes, and give yourself the opportunity to deepen your investment—and the return on it—over time.

Taking a Sabbatical

While mini-lives and part-time endeavors are great for most people, you may find that at some point in your life you have the flexibility to take a sabbatical or an extended break from your job. Doing so allows you to change up your routine and escape the humdrum of daily life for a few weeks or even a few months. While many companies offer their employees the opportunity to take an extended break, a sabbatical doesn't always come at your choosing. It might happen because you lose your job, your contract ends, or you find yourself in transition for some other reason.

Depending on considerations such as your severance package or unemployment benefits, you might be able to make lemonade out of the lemons you've been handed by financing your sabbatical with someone else's dime. The key to making an extended break from work feasible is to first ask yourself a fundamental question: Do you have the resources, both financial and emotional, to make this a worthwhile experience? If you do, then a sabbatical can allow you to hit the pause button before embarking on the next phase of your life.

Once you resolve to take a sabbatical, you next need to decide how you're going to spend your time. If you're not careful, it's shockingly easy to spend some or all of your life in either pajamas or workout clothes, your days filled with a series of frivolous pursuits. For some people, that's the end of the story. After a few months of funemployment, they are sun-tanned, gym fit, and ready to start the first day of their new job. I can't blame them. It's pretty nice to look in the mirror every day and see a rested and healthy face looking back at you. You become the envy of all your friends and get a taste of what it might be like to be one of the idle rich, say the son of a Greek shipping magnate or the daughter of some landed German baron. The irony, of course, is that like anything else, playing the role of idle rich can lose its luster. How many days can you sit around the local café reading the paper, how many miles can you run, and how many nights can you stay out until 3:00 a.m.?

Ideally then, a sabbatical should be used to accomplish two high-level objectives. First, it should serve as a period of restoration, in which the stresses, traumas, and fears of some prior period are suddenly gone, and you can restore both order and balance to your life. As you take a break from your old routines, you will come to a point where you redis-cover the sense of possibility and spirit of adventure that may have been quashed by long hours of work, failed projects, or career disappoint-ments. Second, it should provide a road map toward changing your life for the better in ways that will endure. At some point, you are going to get another job, you are going to work again, and you are going to have new successes and failures, both personal and professional. Following your FOMO to try something you've always wanted to experience can provide you with experiences that will make the next set of adventures in your life considerably richer than they might have been.

Will Wolf's decision to follow his FOMO and take a sabbatical not only helped him to upgrade his résumé—it also launched him into the next phase of his career. Two years ago, Will decided that after a few years working as a data scientist following college, it was time to upgrade his technical skills. He wanted to build additional expertise in machine learning, a field of computer science that gives computers the ability to learn without being explicitly programmed. In the past decade, the discipline has been the force behind self-driving cars, practical speech recognition, effective recommendation engines, and vastly improved fraud detection. Will believed that by increasing his proficiency in the subject, he could join the ranks of technologists who are enabling computers to solve important real-world problems.

A natural next step to achieve this objective would have been graduate school, yet before taking the predictable path, Will asked himself whether he should consider an alternative approach. Graduate school would be an investment of several years and at least $80,000. Furthermore, since the field of machine learning is changing at a blistering pace, he worried that the curriculum available in a university setting would fail to keep up with the labor market. As a result, he decided to blaze his own trail by taking a sabbatical. Will's approach, which he called his Open-Source Machine Learning Masters, was a yearlong self-directed educational deep dive.

All he needed to get going was an internet connection since the resources he would need—online courses, textbooks, academic research, and open-source software materials—were available either online for free or at low cost. Not content with becoming an expert in technology, he also decided he wanted to work on his French as well, so he set off for Casablanca, Morocco. While there, he immersed himself in French, got involved in the local start-up community, and cut his cost of living considerably.

Will's experiment paid off. He spent less than 20 percent of the money he would have invested in a graduate degree, perfected his French, and built a community of friends within the Casablanca entrepreneurship community. He also returned to the workforce from a position of strength. Thanks to all of the connections he made in the machine-learning community as well as a series of fifteen technical blog posts he wrote during his sabbatical, he was inundated with job interviews from the moment he decided to get back to work. Although he didn't have a formal graduate degree, interviewers were wowed by his dedication to learning, his technical skills, and his novel approach to making things happen in his life. He ultimately found a role at an artificial intelligence company that he could not have landed prior to his sabbatical. The increase in pay that came with it made his decision a profitable one.

Finding Freedom from the Fear of Failure

Will, Dan, the Nyamangwanda sisters, and Florencia and her family have all flipped the script to use FOMO for good. They listened to what it was telling them and found ways to integrate unexplored passions and projects into their lives. Most importantly, they took these steps without endangering all of the good things they've got going on in the rest of their lives. That's the upside of having some degree of FOMO. If you know how to use it, it can do a lot of good. You can reconnect with passions and interests that you might have lost touch with over the years. When you were a kid, your hobbies and interests likely played a central role in your life. You didn't even particularly care if you were *good* at them since you did them for the joy of the pursuit. Then over time, you got busy, maybe even a little jaded, and you learned about failure. These factors can combine to hold you back from trying new things and taking risks.

Diego Gonzalez is a twelve-year-old who lives in New York City. Although he's a student by day, he's a 10% Entrepreneur on nights and weekends. He's a remarkable kid, has no fear, and has competed in hackathons, often alongside adults. In fact, he's even won a few prizes, including a free place to work. That's why he's the only twelve-year-old I've ever met who has an office in New York's SoHo neighborhood. When you ask him how he manages his fear of failure, his answer puts things into perspective: "As a kid, I'm not really afraid of failure because if anything does go south then I can still go home, eat some scoops of ice cream and, like, feel normal again." That's the beauty of pursuing something part-time. You don't have to be a kid to see the world as Diego does. Even if you fail, the rest of your life is still there waiting for you, fully intact. You can even have a few scoops of ice cream if you'd like. So while the downside associated with failure is limited, the upside that could come with success is uncapped.

Now that you have learned how to use FOMO for good, it's time to graduate to the final step in dealing with the FOs: you must learn to deal with them in other people. Nothing is more frustrating than overcoming an obstacle in your own life only to realize that you still have to put up with it in the people around you. Thankfully, you do not. You can build upon everything you've learned so far to neutralize other people's FOs, at least as they relate to you. This is the final step in your battle with the FOs, and it only becomes possible now that you fundamentally understand how they work. In the next chapter, you will see how you can manage other people's FOs and even make them work for you.

CHAPTER 14

Game of FOs: Dealing with FOMO and FOBO in Other People

"You may not control all the events that happen to you, but you can decide not to be reduced by them."
—MAYA ANGELOU

When Sam Shank set out to build HotelTonight, he knew that he wanted to stand out from the pack. That was the only way to compete in a very crowded space. From day one, he embraced the mission statement "Plan Less. Live More," and targeted millennials, who are highly mobile, spontaneous, and short in attention span. To achieve this objective, he eschewed the conventional wisdom that has made most online travel agencies carbon copies of each other. Instead of building a website and overwhelming customers with choice, he focused exclusively on a mobile app that offered a limited, yet targeted, assortment of fifteen hotels per night. Perhaps most importantly, he designed the user experience to be frictionless: on the HotelTonight app, you can book a hotel in eight seconds with just three taps. When you compare that with the challenges of booking a trip to Las Vegas discussed in chapter 6, you can understand why Shank raised over $100 million in venture capital before selling the company to Airbnb in 2019.

Shank notes that HotelTonight owes much of its runaway success to the simplicity of its user interface. Since they are asked to choose from a limited number of options, customers can shop without becoming paralyzed by a choice-rich environment. Put another way, they can overcome their FOBO. Of course, if you've ever walked into a Trader Joe's, you know that actively limiting customer choice is not a new concept. Steve Jobs often commented that Apple's entire product line could fit on one table. While that's no longer the case, start-ups like Casper, Farmgirl Flowers, and Harry's have taken up the mantle. For some companies, removing the noise is a core element of their value proposition.

While HotelTonight's design and business model have made great strides at combatting FOBO, the company realized that it needed to do more if it was going to convince even greater numbers of millennials to stop browsing and actually commit. In 2018, the company launched a new feature that was specifically designed to confront FOBO by unleashing its mortal enemy, FOMO. It opted to fight fire with fire in the form of the Daily Drop, a daily deal that's tailored specifically to each client and that offers a 35 percent discount to competitors' prices. Sounds great, right? Well, here's the clincher. You only have fifteen minutes to make a purchase. The offer is ephemeral, so if you don't act during the allotted time, it's gone forever. FOBO, meet FOMO. That's how you play to win in the Game of FOs.

Sam Shank ✓
@samshank

Learned a new acronym today! @HotelTonight's new feature rewards
decisiveness and cures "FOBO" https://quartzy.qz.com/1344485/ via
@qz @rojospinks

July 31, 2018 3:04 PM

When it launched the Daily Drop, HotelTonight was straightforward about its objectives and even pitched the feature as a cure for
FOBO in a social media campaign. While the marketing is clever, it's
the data that tells the real story about what drives consumer behavior:
FOMO clearly vanquishes FOBO when you look at the numbers. The
company has observed a notable spike in bookings immediately after the
customer unlocks the deal and then measures another spike in the last
ten seconds before the offer disappears for good. Moreover, over half
of users who unlock a Daily Drop return again the following week for
another go. They just cannot get enough.

When Someone Else's FOs Become Your Problem

The potential customer who keeps dodging your calls. The boss who
won't commit to a timeline for a promotion. The candidate who won't
give you a definitive response to a job offer. The firm that won't extend
you an offer until you promise to accept. FOMO and FOBO are everywhere. And when they're being used against you, they suck.

Now that you have the tools you'll need to manage your own
FOMO and FOBO, you can also use this knowledge to manage the

FOs in other people. When you're locked in a negotiation, when there is power, reputation, and ego at stake, you have a reasonably good chance of seeing people at their most nakedly self-interested. That means that they are going to show you their FOs. With practice, you'll come to see this as an opportunity, since you can learn to use these behaviors to your advantage. Whenever someone acts like they are Goldilocks and you are The Three Bears, you'll have them right where you want them.

If you want to see the FOs play out in real time, just hang out with an entrepreneur who is looking for capital to grow her business. As the venture capitalist Beth Ferreira taught me years ago, "fundraising isn't about money, it's about power." Founders pitch their idea, paint a picture of a bright and profitable future, and then wait for an answer. If they've done their job, they've told such a compelling story that they've created FOMO. They've used the same tools—social proof, scarcity value, and greed—to unleash the herd that Elizabeth Holmes leveraged so power- fully at Theranos. Hopefully, the outcome will be wildly different.

Investors, on the other hand, see tons of pitches, so it's their job to save their money for the best of the lot. If they invest in just anything, they will deploy all of their capital into lousy companies where they will lose money. Before long, they will be out of business. That's why investors ask endless questions and request as much data as possible. If you're a start-up, you'll hear the same refrain of FOBO from potential investors in nearly every meeting: "I'd love to see a few more months of traction before making a decision." There's a good chance that you'll also hear that very same sentence repeated when you come back in three months to report on your progress. That's a classic investor trope to maintain option value. They continue to ask for more data for as long as they can. Of course, if they're going to have any chance of being successful, they will need to overcome their FOBO and make decisions using a rigorous process like the one you learned about back in chapter 11.

Let's assume that there is mutual interest in getting a deal done. At that point, shouldn't everyone be past their FOs? Hardly. Let's assume that unlike you, the parties at the table have not read this book and remain beholden to their FOs. During the final negotiations, the investor suffers a whole new wave of FOBO as he tries to structure the most favorable deal possible. Meanwhile, seasoned entrepreneurs know that until the money hits their bank account, there's always a chance that an investor will continue to negotiate indefinitely or even walk away. At this point, the company tries to generate another round of FOMO, perhaps by playing one investor against another, in hopes of closing as quickly as possible. One clever strategy that's been used against me (yes, I still struggle with indecision sometimes; I'll admit it) has been for a company to create an exploding offer that expires at a given date. For example, if you fund by the end of the month, the price of the shares is x, but if you fund after that date, the price increases by 20 percent. Entrepreneurs who have used that strategy have told me that they always see a rush of wires coming into the bank the day before the deadline. It's just like the Daily Drop.

Perhaps you read those last few paragraphs and thought to yourself, "Thank God I don't work in that industry. What a bunch of FO'ckers!" Like it or not, *most* commercial interactions work on similar terms. Any time you're trying to sell something, you seek to generate FOMO. Any time you're choosing between various options or trying to get a better deal, you can easily fall victim to FOBO. Ironically, even the process of writing a book about FOMO and FOBO is fraught with both of them. As an author, I needed to generate FOMO from agents and publishers to get them to put a deal on the table. Meanwhile, I heard more than one agent fall victim to FOBO and say, "You're woooonderful and I'd love to sign you. I'm not ready to commit today, but make sure you come back to me before you sign with somebody else."

Peacefully Disarming *FOMO Sapiens* and *FOBO Sapiens*

As you can see, if you think that managing your own FOs can be trying, just wait until you have to put up with somebody else's issues. Fear not. As Carl Jung, he of the wounded healer, notes, "Knowing your own darkness is the best method for dealing with the darknesses of other people."[1]

When it comes to dealing with FOMO and FOBO in others, there is a clear distinction between the two conditions. To be brutally honest, someone else's FOMO isn't really your problem. If a *FOMO sapiens* chooses to invest their time and energy chasing down all the things that they don't want to miss, your best bet may be to stay out of their way. You might even consider using all of that enthusiasm to your advantage. This person will clearly be the first one to respond to your video the next time the ALS Association does the Ice Bucket Challenge. If you're trying to sell them something or get them to take action, you also can deploy some of the tricks laid out in chapter 6 to achieve your objective. That's how you get someone to focus on the things that are important to you, even if that person is all over the place. Of course, if you believe that their FOMO is truly harmful, you can share the strategies in this book with them and get them started on the road to self-awareness and recovery.

The case is quite different, however, when you observe FOMO in the herd, such as in the financial markets. In that case, you have no responsibility to try to save anyone—it would be impractical to do so—but you can potentially profit off the stampede. When you spot the masses chasing after an investment that makes no sense, you don't have to sit on the sidelines shaking your head in disbelief. Instead, you can run in the other direction. Investors large and small have made fortunes betting against the whims of the herd. They spot an overvalued asset, like an overpriced stock, and then short it. While making such a wager entails clear risks, if you do your research and have conviction that you're right—and that all of those *FOMO sapiens* are wrong—then you can position yourself to take the other side of the trade. If you know what you're doing, the potential for huge upside is extraordinary. If you don't believe me, just read *The Big Short*.

While choosing to entangle yourself in someone else's FOMO is entirely optional, dealing with their FOBO, on the other hand, is very much your problem. Their hedging, indecisiveness, and optimizing can exert huge costs on all of the people around them, including you. Whether you pay the price in terms of lost time, lost money, or lost confidence, you shouldn't have to deal with their lack of conviction. It's stressful, annoying, and a huge waste of time. Life's too short to deal with other people's baggage. There are two ways to deal with these people: you can either cut them off or you can learn how to deal with them by neutralizing their FOBO.

First, you can stop dealing with them entirely. People with FOBO are unreliable, they make your life more difficult, and they won't be there when you need them in return. It's completely reasonable to decide that it's better to cut ties now before you find that out the hard way. Rather than upsetting the apple cart or causing conflict, it's best to back away slowly, accepting the fact that you're probably not going to change their behavior absent some major revelation. In the meantime, you will waste time and energy and endure a lot of toxicity in your dealings with them. If you back away slowly, things will probably be just fine. They'll be too caught up in their FOBO to notice you're gone. You won't miss the narcissism, the incessant changing of plans, and the general lack of respect, either.

If cutting ties is not possible or you really want to try to make things work, then your second option is to try to rehabilitate them. While this is technically possible, doing so requires brutal honesty. You need to call out FOBO when you see it, set clear terms for decision-making, demand greater transparency in your relationship, and remain vigilant for relapses. You must also behave in a manner that is beyond reproach when it comes to your own FOBO. It's pretty hard to call someone out when you're just as guilty as they are.

One of the clear areas where you can actually help someone to overcome FOBO is to identify what I call their FOBO crutch. The FOBO crutch is the go-to excuse that this person uses to justify their behavior. This could include such perennial favorites as "I have to work," "The baby is cranky," or "I have to walk the dog." Any of these might be true once in a while, but if you pay attention, you'll notice that *FOBO sapiens* always rely on the same crutches to justify their actions. If you're keen to help someone break out of this cycle, you can start by addressing the issue head-on. Ask them how they plan to avoid any issues with work, the baby, or the dog, and then let them give you the answer. In doing so, you are taking away their crutch and asking them to walk on their own two feet.

When you're dealing with someone who has FOBO, there is a cardinal rule that you must follow to maintain your own sanity: leave no room for choice. In order to address the root cause of their behavior, you must not provide them with a choice-rich environment. Quite the opposite, you will discard all other options so that they face scarcity in their interactions with you. To achieve this objective, you should make all arrangements in advance and put all plans or commitments in writing. You should also be self-interested. Only make plans that you would follow through with on your own in any case. You may also consider offering them specific options that require an immediate response, sort of like your own Daily Drop, so that you aren't left waiting for a commitment. If you follow that playbook, you will never be angry or disappointed when a *FOBO sapiens* flakes, tries to change plans, or equivocates. You've made your plans and you're sticking with them.

If you're dealing with FOBO in a commercial relationship, you can also take inspiration from my acupuncturist Richard Baran, who has managed to eliminate FOBO from his client base. That's pretty amazing in a place like New York City where people ghost, flake, and reschedule almost instinctively. Richard's secret is simple but powerful: if you flake on him, you'll find that it's surprisingly hard to get on his calendar again. As a very successful and in-demand professional, he doesn't lack for clients, so he doesn't have to deal with people who aren't respectful and don't follow the rules. It's a little tough, but it works. As a patient, I now know how important it is to respect his time. Whenever I refer someone new to Richard, I first sit them down and explain to them that if he has to deal with their FOBO, there will be repercussions. While he would never stick you with a needle just to make it hurt, he'll do something worse. He won't stick you with any needles at all because he won't give you an appointment.

While directly tackling someone else's FOBO can be powerful, you cannot, as they say, put lipstick on a pig without facing the consequences. First, if all of the potential options are unattractive, particularly the one that you offer as the only choice, no amount of coaxing, pressure, or intransigence will fix a fundamental problem: indecision, despite all of its negative implications, is still better than affirmatively choosing something that you know is wrong, bad, or disastrous. Second, if you do not control the environment in which you are operating, you can lose control of the decision-making process along with your ability to shape it.

Theresa May tried everything to get Britain's parliament to abandon its FOBO and vote for her Brexit plan, including several of the strategies included in this chapter. First, she stripped down all of the options to one central plan that she tried to sell to the nation. Second, she waited until the very last minute, as close to the original deadline as she could, to call for votes on her plan. Her attempts at a Daily Drop ratcheted up the pressure on lawmakers to vote in her favor, lest the country crash out of the EU without a deal. Still, despite her best efforts, she lost vote after vote, faced a mutiny from her own party, and was condemned to go hat in hand to the European Council to ask for multiple extensions. Her mistake? She failed to remember that FOBO occurs when you are choosing from a number of acceptable options. If you don't have such options, you cannot cure FOBO. Unfortunately for her, as the clock ticked and the deadline approached, it became clear that there was no consensus. As a result, the number of possible acceptable alternatives declined precipitously, and the entire exercise shifted from one of selecting a reasonable path to one of damage control and FODA.

No matter how badly you suffer from FOMO or FOBO or how annoying it is to deal with those qualities in others, bear this in mind: if you have either of the FOs, that means that you have options in the first place. While those options may cause you stress or drive confusion, they are options, no matter how you cut it. As you'll see in the epilogue, if some or all of your options suddenly disappear, you may find out the hard way that you took them for granted.

We're Lucky to Have Options in the First Place

"Remembering that I'll be dead soon is the most important tool I've ever encountered to help me make the big choices in life."
—STEVE JOBS

The air was hot and dry as we drove up to a makeshift camp that blended in surprisingly well with the small village in the Bekaa Valley. It was the summer of 2017, and I was in Beirut for a conference. I had been following the civil war in Syria with increasing concern, and I was troubled by the refugee crisis that it had spawned. I wondered if there was a way to witness this evolving tragedy firsthand, so I asked friends at relief organizations if they could arrange for me to visit some of the Syrian refugee camps that had sprung up in eastern Lebanon. I was hesitant—I had been warned that there might be Hezbollah influence in the camps—but I was assured that my guides, a Lebanese graduate student and a Palestinian who worked for a local NGO, would take care of me.

Our host in the camps was Farid, a lawyer from Aleppo, who now served as the de facto community leader, or *shawish*, and owned a small convenience store on the premises. To my surprise, the conditions were somewhat better than I expected, at least on the surface. The structures were quite basic from the outside, but inside most were tidy, even cheerful. Many of these "homes" belonged to people who were once part of the middle class, people who had lived in apartments and houses back in Syria. Although they had lost nearly everything, they made the most of what they still had at their disposal. The human capacity to adapt to just about anything is astounding.

We spent the day knocking on doors and chatting with families around the camp. At every stop, I was invariably welcomed with an offer of something to eat or drink—coffee, Fanta, sliced watermelon, or a stick of gum. With each conversation, I came to realize that things were far from tidy below the surface. These families, most of which had been refugees for over five years, had no safety net. They were so vulnerable. I visited a three-year-old with leukemia whose only option for treatment was to turn to Doctors Without Borders. A few houses down, I met a man who fell while working on a construction site, severing his spinal cord. He lay in the blistering heat while his wife, surrounded by three small children, told us he could no longer work and that she would have to find a way to pay the bills.

At the root of all of these stories was a common theme: the life of each and every person was frozen, suspended in time until they could somehow escape, whether to another country or back home. While everyone talked about the past and the present, no one talked about the future. What was the point? The only person who openly betrayed a wish for a better tomorrow was a teenager named Mohammed. Lying on the floor and surrounded by his mother and sisters, he fiddled with the smartphone in his hand and confessed with shy enthusiasm that his dream was to become a programmer. I felt a twinge of hope until Farid told me that Mohammed hadn't attended school regularly in years. His family needed him to work full-time picking crops in the fields. Like everyone else in the camp, he had no options.

When I got back to my air-conditioned hotel room that evening, I passed out for a few hours. When I awoke, I felt mentally exhausted and depressed by what I had witnessed. As I stared up at the ceiling, I was reminded of something I had heard back in business school. On the last day of the semester, each professor gives a capstone speech that imparts a bit of wisdom to the students in their class. One professor, in particular, was legendary. First, he pointed out that the population of the earth was eclipsing seven billion people. Then, he urged everyone to appreciate the gifts that they enjoyed in their everyday lives and to contemplate how luck and circumstance had powerfully shaped their destinies. In the final moments of the class, he suggested that each time they felt upset, angry, or frustrated, they should never forget a simple fact: on their worst day, their very worst day, they would still be able to find billions of people who would be willing to trade places with them.

A significant percentage of people in the world will never have to worry about FOMO and FOBO. In order to have FOBO, you must have options. In order to have FOMO, you have to see what you are missing out on and believe that it could somehow be possible for you. When you boil them down to their essence, both FOMO and FOBO are afflictions of abundance. They require you to believe that you have options in life and that you could explore those opportunities under the right circumstances. That is clearly not true for everybody. You don't have to go to Lebanon to meet people who have few to no options in life. You've surely seen it in your own community and perhaps even among your own friends and family. Whether due to illness, poverty, war, repression, or lack of opportunities, when you are marginalized, life is devoid of choices.

Now contrast that harsh reality with how life looks for the privileged few who, by the nature of their achievements, their background, and perhaps their birth, live in an extraordinarily choice-rich environment. It should not be too surprising that such people enjoy far more autonomy and leverage than others in society. That's always been the case. If you're a king or a captain, a CEO or a celebrity, you travel through life in first class while the rest of the world flies coach. Of course, you don't have to be the leader of a country or a movie star to enjoy the benefits that come with privilege. If you're even relatively affluent, you can afford to acquire many more experiences or products than a person of modest means. If you're hyperintelligent and driven, you will tend to have a broader range of professional opportunities. If you're good-looking and have a sparkling personality, you will have an abundance of choices when it comes to dating. None of these things are bad. There's nothing wrong with being born on third base or making the most of what you've got.

The irony, of course, is that despite all of the arrows in your quiver, you may well end up in a very similar place to all those people who are facing a scarcity of choices. When you live in a choice-rich environment, you can end up frozen, suspended in time, due to your own indecision. The difference, of course, is that when you're operating in a choice-rich environment, this is a self-inflicted condition. It's fed by your environment, but if you choose not to fight it, then it's yours and you own it. It is also a circumstance that anyone in that refugee camp would willingly take on if they could. While their universe of alternatives has been shrinking, it seems like most everybody else is increasingly drowning in choice.

In the summer of 2019, I returned to the home of FOMO. Exactly fifteen years after I first wrote about FOMO in the school newspaper, I was back on the campus of HBS for spring reunions. It was a whirlwind of a weekend, packed with so many lectures, parties, and friends that I was instantly reminded of why I wrote that article in the first place. I felt the pull of FOMO as I hadn't in years, as did many of my classmates. The difference was that this time I actively sought to combat it. Knowing that it would only serve to distract me, hijack my attention, and squander the limited time I had back on campus, I opted for focus and conviction instead. Did I miss out on anything? Probably. But I've gotten more comfortable with the fact that I cannot do it all, so I didn't even try. That was the choice I made, and I did so decisively.

Of all of the choices you face, perhaps the most important is to learn to be decisive. If you resolve to do so as you conquer your FOs, you will notice that something magical happens. You escape the little voices in your head that cause you to run in circles when what you really should do is set a course and run in that direction. You then start to think outside of yourself, replacing "me" with "we." You also stop seeing the world as one fixed pie and no longer obsess about maximizing your slice. When you move through the world with clarity, you appreciate your options and gain the confidence to see that there is plenty to go around. Absent all the stress and indecision, these options instead spark gratitude. Each represents a golden opportunity to make the best decisions for yourself, your family, your friends, and your community.

Remember, if your freedom is limited by FOMO and FOBO, life is passing you by. At some point, no matter who you are or how many options you have at your disposal, you cannot live forever, and you cannot take anything with you. For that reason alone, time is of the essence. Unlike the billions of people who have few options, if any, due to war, poverty, or illness, you have plentiful options to change your life and live decisively. You can shape your destiny, fitting it to the contours of your dreams and the demands of reality. You may not get everything you want, but the mere fact that you have the power to try is powerful. It's a gift. Make the most of it. Don't miss out.

Let's Stay in Touch

If there is one thing that still gives me FOMO, it's the notion that anyone who reads this book might have questions, comments, opinions, or solutions that they would be willing to share with me. That's why I would like to invite you to continue the conversation at patrickmcginnis.com. There you will find an updated list of resources on all things FOMO and FOBO as well as a free workbook to accompany this book. I also want to hear from you. You can connect with me in the following ways:

Instagram: @patrickjmcginnis
Twitter: @pjmcginnis
Facebook: PatrickJMcGinnis
Email: letsconnect@patrickmcginnis.com
LinkedIn: linkedin.com/in/patrick-mcginnis

Finally, I invite you to listen to the *FOMO Sapiens* podcast. On the show, you will meet leaders in business, politics, and culture and learn how they choose from among the many opportunities and options in their busy lives. Episodes are available at patrickmcginnis.com/fomosapiens.

Acknowledgments

After writing *The 10% Entrepreneur*, I never really believed that I would write another book, since I had no idea what I would write about. Then, slowly but surely, interactions with readers, friends, and even strangers convinced me that FOMO could be a great topic. I remember the moment when I thought, *Yes, I'm going to do this!*—it was at an Endeavor Global event in Beirut when I took one particularly memorable selfie—and I haven't looked back since. The lesson in all of this? Sometimes, the world conspires to give you your best ideas, so make sure you keep an ear to the ground and listen!

This book wouldn't have been possible had I not found my voice on the *FOMO Sapiens* podcast.

First, I must first thank *Harvard Business Review*, which has been an amazing partner. I owe a huge debt of gratitude to Nitin Nohria, Adi Ignatius, and Adam Buchholz for bringing *FOMO Sapiens* back to *HBS* through the *HBR* community. Of course, if it weren't for Irina Babushkina, none of that would have happened! I am also grateful to Advertising Week, particularly Doug Rowell, Richard Larsson, Alexis Cardoza, and Lance Pillersdorf, for their support in launching *FOMO Sapiens* back in 2018.

FOMO Sapiens would be nowhere without all the guests who have appeared on the show, including Ryan Williams, Sally Wolf, Dorie Clark, Nir Eyal, Khe Hy, Jack Carlson, Jill Carlson, Vicky Hausman, Sisun Lee,

Craig Dubitsky, Kate Eberle Walker, Rip Pruisken, Marco De Leon, Vana Koutsomitis, Diego Gonzalez, Cheryl Einhorn, Andrew Yang, Shan-Lyn Ma, Anu Duggal, Tim Herrera, Eglantina Zingg, Eric Wind, Giancarlo Pitocco, Luke Holden, Galyn Bernard, Christina Carbonell, Jen Wong, Matt Scanlon, Katie Rosman, Bronson van Wyck, Daniella Ballou-Aares, Jamie Metzl, Dr. David Fajgenbaum, Christina Stembel, Will Cole, Oren Klaff, Dr. Darria Long Gillespie, Annastasia Seebohm, Dr. Andrew Kuper, Cathy Heller, Nas Yassin, Meredith Golden, and Beth Ferreira.

Finally, several friends have given me invaluable ideas and insights during the ideation stage of *FOMO Sapiens*: Jeremy Streich, Rasheen Carbin, Nick Martell, and Jack Kramer, your ideas were invaluable to me.

Writing a book is a multiyear process, and I'm always amazed that seemingly innocuous conversations end up serving as the basis for important ideas that eventually find their way into the manuscript. I am eternally grateful to the people who served as sounding boards, brainstorming partners, and sources of ideas for this book. They include Nicole Campbell, Aziz Sunderji, Eric Kroll, Tom Baldwin, Yael Melamed, Diego Saez-Gil, Michael Rogan, Peter Leiman, Arianna Huffington, Scott Stanford, Ajay Kishore, Tristan Mace, Sam Shank, Andrew Watson, Richard Baran, Mariam Malik Alsikafi, Charles Gepp, Claire Marwick, Susan Segal, Dr. Darria Long Gillespie, Stephen Pittman, Jo Tango, Meghann Curtis, Florencia Jimenez-Marcos, Xavier Gonzalez-Sanfeliu, Cecilia Gonzalez-Jimenez, Will Wolf, the Nyamangwanda sisters (Matipa, Mercy, and Maona), Dan Brendtro, and Raena Brendtro.

I wrote this book in New York City and Mexico City, and I did a lot of my best work at coffee shops. I want to thank the teams at Blend Station in Mexico City and Rebel Coffee (with a special shout-out to

Juno, Anthony, and Steph) in NYC who kept me caffeinated as I hogged their tables for hours on end.

Writing is often lonely, but I've always felt like I am surrounded by amazing people who believe in me. I owe a debt of gratitude to some truly remarkable friends who have been a constant source of support and inspiration: Jason Haim, Laura Haim, Michele Levy, John Leone, Dan Mathis, Fraser Simpson, Geoff Gougion, Kathy Gougion, Thomas Gougion, Irene Hong Edwards, Danielle Hootnick, Stewart Oldfield, Mary Oldfield, Greg Prata, Margaret Chu, Tom Clark, Finley Clark, Mildred Yuan, Xin Zeng, Shanthi Divakaran, Nicolas Duleroy, Laura Maydon, Nihar Sait, Brad Saft, Samara O'Shea, Suken Shah, Phil Tseng, Guillermo Silberman, the entire crew from The Wobbly H, Debora Spar, Chava Kallberg, Alicia Doukeris, Juan Navarro-Staicos, Amir Nayeri, Ali Rashid, Jeff Thelen, and Benjamin Spener.

I couldn't do any of this without the team at Motion Ave: Samuel Klein, Alejandra Vasquez, Maria Angelica Quiroz, Rebecca Wigandt, Alexandra Ramirez, Edgar Guillen, and Rosana Toro. I appreciate everything you do enormously. The same goes to you Suzanne Moskowitz— your advice has been consistently helpful.

I am so thankful to my agent, Alice Martell, who is a force of nature and has been a source of ideas, energy, support, and so much more… and I must thank Nick Martell (again!) for introducing me to your mom. What a family!

I am also very grateful for Meg Gibbons, my editor at Sourcebooks, who completely "got it" from the outset and then made this book so much better during the editorial process. Sourcebooks is the perfect place for this book, and when I'm working with the team at Sourcebooks, I have zero FOMO!

Of course, I wouldn't be here at all without Ben Schreckinger (again!) who wrote that first fateful article about the origins of FOMO in *Boston* magazine. I am eternally grateful for your curiosity, for your talent as a writer, and, now, for your friendship.

I also wouldn't even know what FOMO feels like had I not studied at Harvard Business School. Thank you to the Class of 2004 for giving me FOMO and FOBO in the first place.

Finally, I am particularly thankful to my brother, Mike McGinnis, who composed the theme for *FOMO Sapiens* and is just about the best brother you could ever want. Same goes to you, Davalois Fearon, and the consistently amazing Pepper Irie McGinnis. Of course, Mom (my very first editor) and Dad (a.k.a. "The Man Who Knew No FOMO"), we wouldn't be here without you, your support, and your magical ability to help us to make sense of it all and stay grounded.

Notes

Chapter 1

1   Kerry Miller, "Today's Students: Living Large," *Bloomberg Businessweek*, April 8, 2007, https://www.bloomberg.com/news/articles/2007-04-08/todays-students -living-large.

2   Philip Delves Broughton, *Ahead of the Curve: Two Years at Harvard Business School*, (New York: Penguin Press, 2008), 64.

3   Blanca García Gardelegui, "Generación 'fomo,'" *El País*, June 24, 2018, https:// elpais.com/elpais/2018/06/24/opinion/1529859093_682643.html.

4   Shikha Shaa, "Is FOMO Making You Paranoid?" *The Times of India*, January 11, 2013, https://timesofindia.indiatimes.com/life-style/relationships/love-sex/Is -FOMO-making-you-paranoid/articleshow/17730492.cms.

5   Valérie de Saint-Pierre, "Le fomo, nouvelle maladie du siècle?" Madame, *Le Figaro*, January 26, 2015, http://madame.lefigaro.fr/societe/gare-au-digital-bovary sme-160115–93797.

6   Sağlık Haberleri, "Hastalığın adı 'FOMO'! Siz de yakalanmış olabilirsiniz…" *Sabah*, January 10, 2019, https://www.sabah.com.tr/saglik/2019/01/10/fomo ya-yakalanan-kisinin-tedavi-edilmesi-gerekiyor.

Chapter 2

1　　Nick Bilton, "Exclusive: The Leaked Fyre Festival Pitch Deck Is Beyond Parody," *Vanity Fair*, May 1, 2017, https://www.vanityfair.com/news/2017/05/fyre-festival -pitch-deck.

2　　Jaimie Seaton, "Millennials Are Attending Events in Droves Because of Fear of Missing Out," Skift.com, July 12, 2017, https://skift.com/2017/07/12 /millennials-are-attending-events-in-droves-because-of-fear-of-missing-out/.

3　　*Fyre: The Greatest Party That Never Happened*, directed by Chris Smith, Library Films, Vice Studios/Jerry Media, 2019, Netflix, https://www.netflix.com/title /81035279.

4　　"Walmart Unveils Plans for Best Black Friday Yet," Walmart, November 8, 2018, https://news.walmart.com/2018/11/08/walmart-unveils-plans-for-best-black -friday-yet.

5　　Phil Wahba, "Black Friday Fatigue? 174 Million Americans Disagree," *Fortune*, November 28, 2017, http://fortune.com/2017/11/28/black-friday-shopping/.

6　　Daphne T. Hsu et al., "Response of the μ-opioid System to Social Rejection and Acceptance," *Molecular Psychiatry* 18 (August 2013): 1211–1217, https://doi .org/10.1038/mp.2013.96.

7　　Harley Tamplin, "40 Kids Eat World's Hottest Pepper and End Up Needing Medical Treatment," *Metro*, September 5, 2016, https://metro.co.uk/2016/09/05 /emergency-services-called-to-school-after-40-kids-eat-one-of-the-worlds- hottest-peppers-6109851/.

8　　Ann Arens et al., "Esophageal Rupture After Ghost Pepper Ingestion," *The Journal of Emergency Medicine* 51, no. 6 (December 2016): e141–e143, https://doi .org/10.1016/j.jemermed.2016.05.061.

9　　Jacqueline Howard, "Americans Devote More Than 10 Hours a Day to Screen Time, and Growing," CNN.com, July 29, 2016, http://www.cnn.com/2016/06/30 /health/americans-screen-time-nielsen/index.html.

10 Mary Meeker, *Internet Trends Report 2018*, Kleiner Perkins, May 30, 2018, https://www.kleinerperkins.com/perspectives/internet-trends-report-2018.

11 Andrew Perrin and Jingjing Jiang, "About a Quarter of U.S. Adults Say They Are 'Almost Constantly' Online," Pew Research Center, March 14, 2018, http://www.pewresearch.org/fact-tank/2018/03/14/about-a-quarter-of-americans-report-going-online-almost-constantly/.

12 Asurion, "Americans Equate Smartphone Access to Food and Water in Terms of Life Priorities," August 6, 2018, https://www.asurion.com/about/press-releases/americans-equate-smartphone-access-to-food-and-water-in-terms-of-life-priorities/.

13 Samantha Murphy, "Report: 56% of Social Media Users Suffer from FOMO," Mashable.com, July 9, 2013, http://mashable.com/2013/07/09/fear-of-missing-out/.

14 Worldwide Social Network Users: eMarketer's Estimates and Forecast for 2016–2021, https://www.emarketer.com/Report/Worldwide-Social-Network-Users-eMarketers-Estimates-Forecast-20162021/2002081/.

15 Evan Asano, "How Much Time Do People Spend on Social Media?" SocialMediaToday.com, January 4, 2017, https://www.socialmediatoday.com/marketing/how-much-time-do-people-spend-social-media-infographic.

16 Derek Thompson, "How Airline Ticket Prices Fell 50% in 30 Years (and Why Nobody Noticed)," *The Atlantic*, February 28, 2013, https://www.theatlantic.com/business/archive/2013/02/how-airline-ticket-prices-fell-50-in-30-years-and-why-nobody-noticed/273506/.

Chapter 3

1 The FOMO Factory, "Austin's First Selfie Experience Extends Run with New Installations and Overnight Camp," press release, October 10, 2018, https://static1.squarespace.com/static/5b022c2f31d4df352878a8ca/t/5bbe1ee0e5e5f0c3326aa58e/1539186401867/FOMO+FACTORY+-+EXTENSION.pdf.

2   "Fomo," Urbandictionary.com, submitted by Johnny FOMO on September 3, 2013, https://www.urbandictionary.com/define.php?term=fomo&page=4.

3   Katie Heaney, "'Frumbled' and Other Good Reasons to Make Up Words," The Cut, *New York* magazine, January 15, 2019, https://www.thecut.com/2019/01/this -study-on-russian-blues-broke-my-brain.html?utm_source=tw&utm_campaign =nym&utm_medium=s1.

4   Romeo Vitelli, "The FoMo Health Factor: Can Fear of Missing Out Cause Mental and Physical Health Problems?" *Psychology Today*, November 30, 2016, https:// www.psychologytoday.com/blog/media-spotlight/201611/the-fomo-health-factor.

5   Vitelli, "The FoMo Health Factor."

6   Marina Milyavskaya et al., "Fear of Missing Out: Prevalence, Dynamics, and Consequences of Experiencing FOMO," *Motivation and Emotion* 42, no. 5 (October 2018): 725–737, https://doi.org/10.1007/s11031-018-9683-5.

7   Maša Popovac and Lee Hadlington, "Exploring the Role of Egocentrism and Fear of Missing Out on Online Risk Behaviours among Adolescents in South Africa," *International Journal of Adolescence and Youth* (May 2019), https://doi.org/10.108 0/02673843.2019.1617171.

8   Milyavskaya et al., "Fear of Missing Out: Prevalence...", p. 736.

9   "Study: Millennials Want Experiences More Than Anything," *Eventbrite* (blog), December 8, 2014, https://wphub.eventbrite.com/hub/uk/millennials-want -experiences-ds00/.

10   Andrew K. Przybylski et al., "Motivational, Emotional, and Behavioral Correlates of Fear of Missing Out," *Computers in Human Behavior* 29, no. 4 (July 2013): 1841– 1848, p. 1847, https://doi.org/10.1016/j.chb.2013.02.014.

11   Przybylski et al., "Motivational, Emotional, and Behavioral Correlates ..."

Chapter 4

1   Tim Herrera, "How to Make Tough Decisions Easier," *New York Times*, June 4, 2018, https://www.nytimes.com/2018/06/04/smarter-living/how-to-finally-just -make-a-decision.html?module=inline.

Chapter 5

1   Sylvia Plath, *The Bell Jar* (United Kingdom: Heinemann, 1963): 80.

2   Barry Schwartz, *The Paradox of Choice: Why More Is Less* (New York: Ecco, 2004): 77.

3   Schwartz, *The Paradox of Choice*, 78.

4   H. R. Markus and Barry Schwartz, "Does Choice Mean Freedom and Well -Being?" *Journal of Consumer Research* 37, no. 2 (2010): 344–355, https://works.swarth more.edu/fac-psychology/5/.

5   David Brooks, "The Golden Age of Bailing," opinion, *New York Times*, July 7, 2017, https://www.nytimes.com/2017/07/07/opinion/the-golden-age-of-bailing .html.

Chapter 6

1   Jennifer Pak, "FOMO in China Is a $7 Billion Industry," *Marketplace*, September 13, 2018, https://www.marketplace.org/2018/09/13/world/fomo-china-7-billion -industry.

2   Pak, "FOMO in China is a $7 Billion Industry."

3   Li Xiaolai, "From now on, Li Xiaolai will not do any project investment (whether it is a blockchain or not)," trans. by Google Translate, Weibo, September 30, 2018, https://www.weibo.com/1576218000/GBF5rzI2o?filter=hot&root_comment _id=0&type=comment.

4   "Market Capitalization: The Total USD Value of Bitcoin Supply in Circulation,

as Calculated by the Daily Average Market Price Across Major Exchanges,"
Blockchain.com, accessed July 12, 2019, https://www.blockchain.com/en/charts
/market-cap?timespan=all.

5   Alisa Wolfson, "How to Turn Your Pet into a Five-Figure Instagram Influencer,"
New York Post, July 10, 2018, https://nypost.com/2018/07/10/how-to-turn
-your-pet-into-a-five-figure-instagram-influencer/.

6   Matthew Herper, "From $4.5 Billion to Nothing: Forbes Revises Estimated Net
Worth of Theranos Founder Elizabeth Holmes," *Forbes*, June 21, 2016, https://www
.forbes.com/sites/matthewherper/2016/06/01/from-4-5-billion-to-nothing
-forbes-revises-estimated-net-worth-of-theranos-founder-elizabeth-holmes/#83526
a536331.

7   Andrew Bary, "What's Wrong, Warren?" *Barron's*, December 27, 1999, https://
www.barrons.com/articles/SB945992010127068546.

8   Bessemer Venture Partners, "Google," The Anti-Portfolio, accessed May 20, 2019,
https://www.bvp.com/anti-portfolio/.

9   Bessemer Venture Partners, "Facebook," The Anti-Portfolio, accessed May 20,
2019, https://www.bvp.com/anti-portfolio/.

Chapter 7

1   Blair Decembrele, "Your Guide to Winning @Work: FOBO—The Fear of Better
Options," *LinkedIn* (blog), October 5, 2018, https://blog.linkedin.com/2018
/october/5/your-guide-to-winning-work-fobo-the-fear-of-better-options.

2   Matt Singer, "2018 Recruiter Nation Survey: The Tipping Point and the Next
Chapter in Recruiting," Jobvite, November 8, 2018, https://www.jobvite.com
/jobvite-news-and-reports/2018-recruiter-nation-report-tipping-point-and-the
-next-chapter-in-recruiting/.

3   Patrick Gillespie, "Intuit: Gig Economy Is 34% of US Workforce," CNN.com, May

24, 2017, https://money.cnn.com/2017/05/24/news/economy/gig-economy -intuit/index.html.

4   Audi AG, *Annual Reports: 2018*, March 14, 2019, p. 84, https://www.audi.com /en/company/investor-relations/reports-and-key-figures/annual-reports.html.

5   Audi AG, *Annual Reports: 2018*, p. 106.

6   Brad Berman, "Analysis Paralysis: Audi Offers Yet Another Electric Car Study," plugincars.com, November 22, 2011, https://www.plugincars.com/audi-all -electric-a3-e-tron-110332.html.

7   Gil Press, "6 Predictions for the $203 Billion Big Data Analytics Market," *Forbes*, January 20, 2017, https://www.forbes.com/sites/gilpress/2017/01/20/6 -predictions-for-the-203-billion-big-data-analytics-market/#321bfa372083.

8   Bernard Marr, "Big Data: 20 Mind-Boggling Facts Everyone Must Read," *Forbes*, September 30, 2015, https://www.forbes.com/sites/bernardmarr/2015/09/30 /big-data-20-mind-boggling-facts-everyone-must-read/#6b5c806717b1.

9   Quentin Hardy, "Gearing Up for the Cloud, AT&T Tells Its Workers: Adapt, or Else," *New York Times*, February 13, 2016, https://www.nytimes.com/2016/02/14 /technology/gearing-up-for-the-cloud-att-tells-its-workers-adapt-or-else.html.

10 Capgemini Invent (@CapgeminiInvent), "Since 2000, 52% of companies in the Fortune 500 have either gone bankrupt, been acquired, or ceased to exist," Twitter, May 10, 2015, 6:25 p.m., https://twitter.com/capgeminiconsul /status/597573139057537025?lang=en.

11 Lori Ioannou, "A Decade to Mass Extinction Event in S&P 500," CNBC.com, June 5, 2014, https://www.cnbc.com/2014/06/04/15-years-to-extinction-sp-500 -companies.html.

12 Ellen Barry and Benjamin Mueller, "'We're in the Last Hour': Democracy Itself Is on Trial in Brexit, Britons Say," *New York Times*, March 30, 2019, https://www .nytimes.com/2019/03/30/world/europe/uk-brexit-democracy-may.html.

Chapter 8

1   Alfred Duning, "The Return of the *Resolute*," *American Heritage* 10, no. 5 (August
     1959), https://www.americanheritage.com/content/return-resolute.

2   Office of the Curator, The White House, "Treasures of the White House: *Resolute*
     Desk," The White House Historical Association, accessed May 20, 2019, https://
     www.whitehousehistory.org/photos/treasures-of-the-white-house-resolute-desk.

Chapter 9

1   "Message of Pope Francis for the Twenty-Ninth World Youth Day 2014," January 21,
     2014,   http://w2.vatican.va/content/francesco/en/messages/youth/documents
     /papa-francesco_20140121_messaggio-giovani_2014.html.

Chapter 10

1   Evan Andrews, "7 Unusual Ancient Medical Techniques," History.com, August 22,
     2018, https://www.history.com/news/7-unusual-ancient-medical-techniques.

Chapter 11

1   Jeffrey Hughes and Abigail A. Scholer, "When Wanting the Best Goes Right
     or Wrong: Distinguishing Between Adaptive and Maladaptive Maximization,"
     Personality and Social Psychology Bulletin 43, no. 4 (February 2017): 570–583,
     https://doi.org/10.1177/0146167216689065.

2   Dan Silvestre, "*The Life-Changing Magic of Tidying Up* by Marie Kondo: Lessons,"
     review of *The Life-Changing Magic of Tidying Up* by Marie Kondo, Medium.com,
     September 7, 2018, https://medium.com/@dsilvestre/the-life-changing-magic
     -of-tidying-up-by-marie-kondo-lessons-d33dc4db73c2.

Chapter 12

1   Luca Ventura, "World's Largest Companies 2018," *Global Finance*, November 30, 2018, https://www.gfmag.com/global-data/economic-data/largest-companies.

2   Sundar Pichai, "Keynote (Google I/O '18)" speech, Google Developers, video, streamed live on May 8, 2018, https://youtu.be/ogfYd705cRs.

3   Nellie Bowles, "Silicon Valley Nannies Are Phone Police for Kids," *The New York Times*, October 26, 2018, https://www.nytimes.com/2018/10/26/style/silicon-valley-nannies.html.

4   Jared Gilmour, "'Addictive' Social Media Should Be Regulated Like Cigarettes, Tech CEO Says," *Ledger-Enquirer*, January 24, 2018, http://amp.ledger-enquirer.com/news/nation-world/national/article196429794.html.

5   Bartie Scott, "Why Meditation and Mindfulness Training Is One of the Best Industries for Starting a Business in 2017," *Inc.*, March 1, 2017, https://www.inc.com/bartie-scott/best-industries-2017-meditation-and-mindfulness-training.html.

6   University of Pennsylvania, "Social Media Use Increases Depression and Loneliness, Study Finds," ScienceDaily.com, November 8, 2018, www.sciencedaily.com/releases/2018/11/181108164316.htm.

7   Asurion, "Americans Equate Smartphone Access to Food and Water in Terms of Life Priorities," August 6, 2018, https://www.asurion.com/about/press-releases/americans-equate-smartphone-access-to-food-and-water-in-terms-of-life-priorities/.

8   Arnie Kozak, PhD, *The Everything Buddhism Book*, 2nd ed. (Avon, MA: Adams Media, 2011): 30.

9   Sundar Pichai, "Keynote (Google I/O '18)" speech, Google Developers, video, streamed live on May 8, 2018, https://youtu.be/ogfYd705cRs.

10 Anil Dash, "JOMO!" *Anile Dash* (blog), July 19, 2012, https://anildash.com/2012/07/19/jomo/.

Chapter 13

1   Katherine Robinson, "Robert Frost: 'The Road Not Taken,'" Poetry Foundation, May 27, 2016, https://www.poetryfoundation.org/articles/89511/robert-frost -the-road-not-taken.

Chapter 14

1   "Carl Gustav Jung," in *Oxford Essential Quotations*, ed. Susan Ratcliffe (Oxford University Press, 2016), https://www.oxfordreference.com/view/10.1093 /acref/9780191826719.001.0001/q-oro-ed4-00006107.

Index

A

activism, 185–187

addiction, 24–25, 110, 163

Amazon, 55–56, 83

analysis paralysis, 93–95

Ansel, Dominique, 75–76

"anti-portfolio," 82–83

Apple, 112, 159, 163

"ask the watch" concept, 120–122

Aspirational FOMO, 14, 71, 72–74, 131–136

asset bubbles, 77–78

AT&T, 96

Audi, 93–94

B

baby boomers, 33

bailing, 57–58

Balwani, Ramesh "Sunny," 78

Baran, Richard, 203

Barron's, 81

Bellas, the (Thorne and Hadid), 11–12

Bell Jar, The (Plath), 48–50

Benioff, Marc, 160

Bessemer Venture Partners, 81–83

Bieber, Justin, 73

"big data," 94–95

biological factors, 18–20, 50–52

bitcoin, 69–71

Black Friday, 15–17, 19

brain, emotional response of, 18–19

Brendtro, Dan, 186–187

Brexit, 98–100, 204

Buddhist meditation, 167–168

Buffett, Warren, 81

C

career, damage to, 87–88

career decisions, 88–90

celebrities. *See* influencers

China, 69–71

choice-rich environment, 53–56, 60, 61–62, 207–209

conscious multitasking, 180, 189

conviction, 106–110

Cronuts, 75–76

crowdfunding, 187

cryptocurrencies, 69–71, 83–84

cultural factors, 20–22, 52–53

Cyrus, Miley Ray, 73

D

Daily Drop, 196–197

Dash, Anil, 172–173

decision-making strategies. See strategies for overcoming FOMO/FOBO

delegating to your squad, 122–126

digital mindfulness, 167–172

digital wellness initiatives, 158–159, 160

Dolan, Frederick, 113–114, 170

Draper, Tim, 79

E

eating challenges, 20–21

electronic devices. See technology

emotional response, 18–19

empowerment, 122–126

EnnyEthnic, 183

entitlement, 43

entrepreneurship FOMO, 180–194

F

Facebook, 82

Fear of a Better Option. See FOBO

Fear of Doing Anything. See FODA

Fear of Missing Out. See FOMO

Fearon, Davalois, 109

fig tree metaphor, 48–50

financial markets, 200–201

FOBO (Fear of a Better Option), xvii, 39–65. See also strategies for overcoming FOMO/FOBO; technology

    as anti-strategy, 85–100

    biological factors, 50–52

    combined with FOMO, xii–xiii, 98–100

    commodification of choice, 53–56

    compared to FOMO, 40

    concept, xii, 39–41

    cultural factors, 52–53

    dealing with, in other people, 195–204

defined, 41–43

holding out for something better,
42, 43–44

life, stages of, 59–62

narcissism, 56–59

preserving option value, 43, 44–45,
95–97

self-assessment questions, 63–64

FOBO crutch, 202

FOBO sapiens, 62–65

focus, 106–110, 156–157

FODA (Fear of Doing Anything),
xiii, 98–100

followers, 73–74, 137

FOMO (Fear of Missing Out),
1–38. *See also* strategies for
overcoming FOMO/FOBO;
technology

Aspirational, 14, 71, 72–74, 131–
136

biological factors, 18–20

combined with FOBO, xii–xiii,
98–100

compared to FOBO, 40

concept, x–xi

cultural factors, 20–22

dealing with, in other people,
195–204

defined, 13, 30

as driver of commerce, 69–84

as force for good (making FOMO
work for you), xvi–xvii, 140,
177–194

Generation FOMO, 32–35

good vs. bad, 178–180

herd mentality, 19, 71–72, 74–77,
136–139

inclusion, role of, 14–15, 71–72

information asymmetry, 14, 130,
131–136, 146

vs. JOMO (Joy of Missing Out),
172–174

life, stages of, 32–35

memes, 29–30

negative effects, xi, 30–32

origin and spread of term, xi, 1–9

perception, role of, 13–14, 71, 130

self-assessment questions, 36–37

technological factors, 6, 22–28

FOMO Factory, The, 29

FOMO sapiens, ix–xi, 35–38

food challenges, 20–21

Foreman, George, 72

freelancing, 89–90

Frost, Robert, 178–179

Fyre Festival, 11–12, 74

G

Generation FOMO, 32–35

Gen Xers, 33

Gen Z, x

ghosting, 40, 58

gig economy, 89–90

goals, achieving your, 188–190

"Goldilocks and the Three Bears,"
85–86

Gomez, Selena, 73

Gonzalez, Diego, 193–194

Google, 82, 158–159, 184–185

Grande, Ariana, 145–146

Great British Bake Off (GBBO),
188

greed, 77–80

gut checks, 136–139

H

H&M, 55

Hadid. *See* Bellas, the

Harvard Business School, 1–4, 5,
209

Herd FOMO, 19, 71–72, 74–77,
136–139

High-Stakes Decisions, 114, 133–
140, 147–153

holding out for something better,
42, 43–44

Holmes, Elizabeth, 78–80

HotelTonight, 195–197

Huffington, Arianna, 166–167

hunter-gatherers, 18, 51

I

inclusion, 14–15, 71–72

inertia, 97–100, 139–140

influencers, 11–12, 14, 72–74, 137

information, access to, 23–25

information asymmetry, 14, 130,
131–136, 146

innovation, 95–97, 184–185

Instagram. *See* social media

internet. *See* technology

intrapreneurship, 184–185

J

Ja Rule, 11–12, 74

Jenner, Kendall, 11–12, 21–22

Jimenez-Marcos, Florencia,
177–178

job market, 88–90

Jobs, Steve, 112

JOMO (Joy of Missing Out),
172–174

K

Kardashian, Rob, 73

Keeping Up with the Joneses
(comic strip), 6, 26

Kondo, Marie (KonMari method),
144–145

L

labor market, 88–90

leadership, 95–100, 103–104, 111–
112, 122–126

life, stages of, 32–35, 59–62

LinkedIn, 89

"Live for Now Moments Anthem"
(Pepsi ad), 21–22

Long Island Iced Tea (Long
Blockchain Corp), 83–84

Low-Stakes and No-Stakes
Decisions, 114–127

M

Ma, Shan-Lyn, 138

marketers, 74–77

maximizers/maximization, 51–53,
142–143

May, Theresa, 100, 204

MBA programs, 4–5

McDonald's, 29

McFarland, Billy, 11–12, 74

meditation/mindfulness, 167–172

Melamed, Yael, 141–142, 146

memes, 29–30

millennials, x, 11–12, 21–22, 32–
35, 166, 195–197

mindfulness, 167–172

N

narcissism, 56–59

No-Stakes and Low-Stakes
Decisions, 114–127

Nyamangwanda, Matipa, Mercy,
and Maona, 183

O

optimizing, 43–44, 95–97

option value, 43, 44–45, 95–97,
141–153

outsourcing, 118–127

P

part-time entrepreneurs, 180–194

passions, exploring your, 188–190

"pay-for-knowledge" products,
    69–70

Pepsi, 21–22, 83

perception, 13–14, 53, 71, 130

Pichai, Sundar, 158–159

Plath, Sylvia, 48–50

portfolio career, 89–90

prioritization, 112–117

productivity, 108

R

Ratajkowski, Emily, 11–12

reference anxiety, 26–28, 129–130

relationships, 40–41, 91–92

Resolute desk, 103–104

risk aversion, 43, 52

"Road Not Taken, The" (Frost),
    178–179

S

sabbaticals, 190–193

Saez-Gil, Diego, 187

satisficers, 52

scarcity value, 75–77

screen time, 23, 160. *See also*
    technology

Segal, Susan, 123–124

self-assessment questions
    for FOBO, 63–64
    for FOMO, 36–37
    for relationship with technology,
        161–163

self-interest, 56–59

Shank, Sam, 195–197

side hustles, 182–183

Silicon Valley, 77–80, 160

sleep problems, 166–167

smartphones. *See* social media;
    technology

social media, x, 160, 165. *See also*
    technology
    Black Friday and, 15–17
    extreme interconnectivity, 25
    FOMO, linked to, 25, 31–32
    FOMO memes, 29–30
    influencers, 11–12, 14, 72–74, 137
    reference anxiety, 26–28
    self-assessment questions, 161–163

social proof, 72, 75–77

Starbucks, 55

start-ups, 97

Stephenson, Randall, 96

strategies for overcoming FOMO/
FOBO, xiv–xv, 103–174. *See also*
technology
  choosing action over option value
    (FOBO), 141–153
  choosing what you actually want, xv,
    107, 112–117
  dealing with FOs, in other people,
    195–204
  eliminating information asymmetry
    in Aspirational FOMO, 131–136
  gut checks to escape the herd,
    136–139
  high-stakes decisions, 114, 133–
    140, 147–153
  low-stakes and no-stakes decisions,
    114–127
  making FOMO work for you, xvi–
    xvii, 140, 177–194
  missing out on the rest, xv, 107,
    155–174
swarm intelligence, 19
Syrian refugee camps, 205–207

T

technology. *See also* social media
  actions for focusing on what mat-
    ters, 156–157

addiction to, 24–25, 163
basic precepts for, 172
battle for your consciousness,
  157–164
digital mindfulness, 167–172
digital wellness initiatives, 158–159,
  160
encroachment on your personal
  space, 158, 166–167
extreme interconnectivity, 25
FOMO and, 6, 22–28
ghosting/bailing, role in, 58
JOMO (Joy of Missing Out) and,
  172–174
reference anxiety, 26–28
relentless access to information,
  23–25
rethinking/reframing your relationship with, 164–167
self-assessment questions, 161–163
10% Entrepreneurs, 182–183,
  193–194
"thank u, next" (song), 145–146
Theranos, 78–80
Thorne. *See* Bellas, the
Tinder, 86–87

U

unicorns, 184

V

venture capitalism, 80, 81–83

W

Walmart, 17
WeWork, 181
wildebeest migration metaphor,
    19–20
Willy Wonka & the Chocolate
    Factory, 47–48
Wolf, Will, 191–193
workplace. *See* labor market
World Economic Forum, 160
wounded healer, xiii

X

Xiaolai, Li, 69–71

Y

"You Only Live Once" (YOLO), 34

Z

ZARA, 55
Zola, 138

About the Author

Patrick J. McGinnis is a venture capitalist, writer, and speaker who has invested in leading companies in the United States, Latin America, Europe, and Asia.

He is the creator and host of the hit podcast *FOMO Sapiens*, which is distributed by *Harvard Business Review*. Patrick coined the term "FOMO," short for "Fear of Missing Out," which was added to the *Oxford English Dictionary* in 2013. He is also the creator of the term "FOBO" or "Fear of a Better Option" and has been featured as the creator of both terms in media outlets including the *New York Times*, *Politico*, *The Financial Times*, *Boston Globe*, *Guardian*, *Inc.* magazine, *Cosmopolitan*, and MSNBC. His TED Talk "How to Make Faster Decisions" was released in 2019.

Patrick is the author of the international bestseller *The 10% Entrepreneur: Live Your Startup Dream Without Quitting Your Day Job*, a guide to part-time entrepreneurship. Translated into over ten foreign languages, the book has been featured by the BBC, MSNBC, CNN en Español, *Entrepreneur*, *Fast Company*, *Forbes*, *Fortune*, and many other media outlets worldwide.

As a 10% Entrepreneur, Patrick has invested in, advised, or founded more than twenty part-time entrepreneurial ventures spanning the high-tech, real estate, and entertainment industries. Two of the companies in his investment portfolio have subsequently become unicorns. He is also an investor in the UK theatrical production of *The Last King of Scotland.*

He is a proud founding member of the Leadership Council at Sesame Workshop and is an avid fan of Grover, who is clearly the Muppet with the most FOMO.

A graduate of Georgetown University and Harvard Business School, Patrick has visited more than one hundred countries and is fluent in Spanish, Portuguese, and French. He lives in New York City.

For more information, visit patrickmcginnis.com.